# NURSE STAFFING & BUDGETING

## *Practical Management Tools*

*Roey Kirk*

AN ASPEN PUBLICATION®
Aspen Publishers, Inc.

1986

Rockville, Maryland
Royal Tunbridge Wells

Library of Congress Cataloging in Publication Data

Kirk, Roey.
Nurse staffing & budgeting.

"An Aspen publication."
1. Nursing service administration. 2. Health facilities—Personnel management.
3. Program budgeting. I. Title. II. Title: Nurse staffing and budgeting.
[DNLM: 1. Nursing Staff, Hospital—organization & administration handbooks. WY 39 K59n]
RT85.K56    1986    362.1'73'068    86-3455
ISBN 0-87189-365-7

Library of Congress Catalog Card Number: 86-3455
ISBN: 0-87189-365-7

Printed in the United States of America

1  2  3  4  5

# Table of Contents

## Section 4: Staffing Pattern Development............................35

## Section 5:  Prospective Budget Control.............................47

## Section 6:  Prescheduling Staff-More Planning Ahead.............63

## Nurse Staffing & Budgeting: Practical Management Tools

Competency and responsibility levels continue to evolve for nurse managers, growing to new levels of sophistication in a dynamic and constantly changing health care industry. With every change and new development, nurse managers who choose to maintain their position and level of involvement grow as well. Granted, there are sometimes growing pains, but sharpened skills, new information sources, and a wealth of different experiences are positive payoffs that have catapulted many nurse managers to levels of managerial competency they may have never thought possible.

Being a competent nurse manager in today's health care industry is more complex and much more demanding than it was ten years ago. As a result, today's practicing nurse managers are hungry for knowledge relating to every aspect of their department. There is an increasing awareness that the best way to optimize patient care while maximizing financial and competitive outcomes is to manage all aspects of the department. Many are seeking, or being offered more authority over many entities for which they have always had some element of responsibility and accountability. With the new control comes the need for back up systems, methods and management tools to help facilitate effective, efficient decision making.

The purpose of this book is to provide these back up systems, methods, and techniques for nurse managers and administrators to help them manage their units, departments, and divisions more effectively and more efficiently with the indirect but ultimate focus on improving patient care. The book is filled with practical management tools that have been used successfully and taught to hundreds of students, managers, and administrators. This book doesn't just tell you how you should do things, it provides forms and formulas that can be copied and implemented immediately. The goal is not to tie up your time recreating an idea from the book, but to give you the opportunity to quickly try an idea and assess its potential application in your organization.

The step-by-step instruction style enables both independent and classroom learning. Practicing nurse managers, administrators and ex-ecutives will find this an excellent resource for new ideas, innovations, and challenges that will help them manage their responsibilities. In addition, key concepts, formulas, and forms have been set up so that educators of nursing management and administration students can easily make overhead transparencies and homework assignments directly from the book examples. Each form and worksheet is set up two ways: (1) the first presentation is an example filled in to show how it is used and is then followed by (2) a blank form that is ready for copying. For those of you who want to revise or personalize the forms, accompanying software, compatible with Apple's Macintosh™ hardware, is available from the author (Roey Kirk Associates, P.O. Box 160309, Miami, FL 33116).

Although the outline of the book follows a process that is best understood when read in order, the text has also been designed to meet the needs of readers who only want to read a particular section. In Section 1, Developing the Unit of Service and Identifying the Department's Standard, the process begins by looking at the nursing department's unit of service-the patient day-as the key factor in managing staffing and budgeting responsibilities. Drawing on information from the patient classification system, the unit of service can be evaluated to identify the average amount of nursing care hours required per patient day on a particular unit.

Once a standard number of nursing care hours per patient day is established, it can be used as the basis of budget planning for the upcoming fiscal year. Section 2, Using Nursing Care Standards for Budget Planning, describes ways to plan and prepare for: (1) budget calculation activities and (2) ongoing quality and productivity monitoring. Section 3, Using the Nursing Care Standard for Budget Calculation, uses the unit standard as the constant factor in the budget. The result is a budget based on patient care needs with built-in flexibility for unexpected variations in both volume and acuity. Following, in Section 4, Staffing Pattern Development, the same unit standard is used to outline a plan for prescheduling staff in a consistent, flexible pattern designed to meet both the needs of the patient and the cost containment goals of the institution.

Section 5, Prospective Budget Control, addresses a variety of internal and external variables that affect budget performance. Many are beyond the control of the nurse manager, but taking a proactive stance by planning ahead through the use of position control, performance management systems, and prehiring agreements can influence outcomes. In the last section, Section 6, Prescheduling Staff-More Planning Ahead, scheduling techniques are used to preschedule staff, the last part of the budget planning process. When staff are prescheduled according to the identified standard nursing care hours per patient day, the nurse manager achieves maximum flexibility in meeting patient care needs by adjusting staff members for actual daily fluctuations in both volume and acuity.

There are literally hundreds to thank, from university students to seminar participants to colleagues. I wish to especially thank two excellent nurse managers, Yvonne Kieval and Joan Karaboyas for being energetic, for always listening with enthusiasm to every crazy new idea I thought of or brought from seminars, for always being the best you could be, and for making my job easy and enjoyable.

# Section 1

# Developing the Unit of Service and Identifying the Department's Standard

## Introduction: Getting Started

Managerial competence is a necessity and a goal of every nurse manager. Many nurse managers entered nursing for altruistic reasons and found that their clinical achievements and competence led to managerial promotions. To these individuals (and others) the reality of today's health care environment can sometimes be awesome, frightening, and frustrating. Nurses provide care, spend the most time with the patient, know them and their families, and are most knowledgeable about the level and quality of care that each patient receives. Often, managing the budget and managing patient care seem to create a conflict in the mind of the nurse manager. However, in today's health care environment of competition and cost containment, managers must be able to manage patient care and productivity in a cohesive and complementary way in order to survive.

To achieve this objective, nurse managers need to know both that quality can be managed and how to do it. Questions about how the manager can measure quality, quantify quality, and ensure quality on a daily basis, to both the patient and the staff, must be posed and answered. Although the questions seem vague and unanswerable, there are specific and simple methodologies that can lead to the answers. Once the quality issue is correctly resolved, the information can be used as the core of the budget and productivity systems.

This workbook contains many ideas, methodologies and even forms that can be copied and used. The surprise is that, as you use them and apply them to your own situation, you may revise or even develop your own new ideas. The combination of experience, imagination, and innovation will separate the leaders of health care from the rest of the pack.

1

# Step #1 - Gathering Data

- Identifying how many labor hours patient care consumes by task can be measured through:

    - Hours per patient day, or
    - Hours per DRG case, or
    - Hours per nursing diagnosis category.

- Tracking the above information on logs or reports provides:

    - Information about changing patterns (seasonal, market share) of resource labor hour consumption.

    - Retrospective data:

        * Nursing intensity (Acuity)
        * Length of stay

- Identifying the volume and diagnostic (DRG or nursing) distribution of current patients provides valuable information to:

    - Rank diagnosis categories to identify heavy users of the department's services by both volume and intensity

    - Identify nursing intensity measures which will update and validate patient care needs on an ongoing basis

# Service Units

The service that a department provides is the foundation of all department activities from program and budget planning to productivity monitoring and evaluation. The **unit of service** is the common denominator that enables identification and measurement of activities in terms of both quality and quantity. Inpatient nursing departments use the **patient day**, with hours per patient day as the time measure; however, units of service for new outpatient nursing services and other entrepreneurial ventures, may begin to look more like the ones in the following chart.

| Department | Service Units | Time Measure* |
|---|---|---|
| Emergency | Total visits | Hours per visit |
| Physical therapy | Treatments (modalities) | Hours per modality |
| Food service | Patient and cafeteria meals<br>Dietician visits | Hours per meal<br>Hours per visit |
| Labor and delivery | Births | Labor minutes per birth |
| Surgery | Major and minor operations | Hours per operation |
| Laboratory | Tests | CAP units<br>(College of American Pathologists) |
| Radiology | Exams or x-rays | Relative value units |
| Housekeeping | Square footage | Weighted square footage |
| Nursing-inpatient | Patient day | Hours per patient day (HPPD) |

* Hours refer to labor or manhours worked to deliver the particular service, on the average. Example: if there were 1,000 visits that took 1 hour of labor time and 1,000 that consumed 30 minutes of labor time, then the average visit would take 45 minutes ( [60 x 1,000] + [30 x 1,000] ÷ 2,000 = 45 ).

# Assigning Time Values to Service Units

When activities of patient care are evaluated to determine the consumption of nursing labor hours, the activities and times can be accumulated and averaged to identify the **standard** nursing care hours required per unit of service, the patient day. In other words, there should be a predetermined decision or allocation of time available for each unit of service. Some examples are given below:

| | |
|---|---|
| 4.0 | Nursing care hours per patient day (med-surg unit) |
| 12.0 | Nursing care hours per patient day (coronary intensive care) |
| 0.5 | Physical therapist hours per patient treatment (modality) |
| .7 | Interdisciplinary hours per ER visit (.3 nursing, .2 physician, .2 other) |

In the past, before the advent of a constrained cost system, the standard hours of care were determined based on what was desirable to give the patient. Now the desire and, indeed, justification may be present to provide that level of care, but the funding is unavailable. Thus, future standards of care may be based not on what is desired or needed for the patient, but rather on what is affordable within the given reimbursement limitation. It will be the challenge of nursing management to create an environment of productivity whereby the desirable level of quality can be maintained under the mandated constraints.

There are several ways to define or develop standards, and it is crucial that once they are approved they are credible and can be validated continuously. Once a standard is validated and deemed reliable it can be used as the focal point of all department financial and quality assurance planning. Should all this planning be done on the basis of an unreliable standard, the results could be significantly damaging, so it is advantageous to research carefully and substantiate the unit standard before putting it to work.

The first step in putting the unit standard to work entails determining the time and quality components. The business of nursing is patient care, and the quality of work is determined by how the consumer evaluates the work, so sufficient time and planning for a workload within that given time are the best ways to achieve the target level of quality.

| | | Labor Hours | | |
|---|---|---|---|---|
| Quality Standards | + | Needed to Meet the Quality Standards | = | Unit of Service **Standard** |

# Determining Standards

A department <u>standard</u> can be developed by (1) defining the measurable levels of quality that are routinely accomplished during the provision of the service and (2) determining the  length of time it takes to do the particular unit of service at the desired level of quality.   There are a number of methods for defining and determining standards for both patient days and outpatient procedures or modalities.  Some of these methods are listed below, with their potential advantages and disadvantages:

| | |
|---|---|
| **Estimating** | The "best guess" approach.  It is low in cost and takes little time, but is biased and not always related to current internal or external conditions. |
| **Historical Averaging** | This is the easiest, least expensive route to take, and for this reason it is generally accepted: but it could be the worst method because it is imprecise and perpetuates any deficiencies or inefficiencies.  Example:  Last year Unit 3N worked 30,000 manhours and accumulated 9,000 patient days.  **30,000 ÷ 9,000 = 3.3** nursing care hours per patient day. |
| **Logging** | Excellent, low cost methodology in which staff members are trained to log the activities they do and the length of time it takes them to do the activities.  Can be used to identify and develop time values needed for patient classification system categories. Logs, such as **Activity Time Log,** Form 1.1, can be used to identify labor time required, on the average, for individual activities.  The logs can then be used to determine total time involvement (1) by classification category,  (2) by nursing care plan, (3) by diagnosis category, or (4) by standards of care. |
| **Work Sampling** | Random instantaneous observations that measure the relative time spent on various work elements, usually by an outside source, such as a consultant, management  engineer, or industrial engineer. |
| **Predetermined** | Industry-accepted standards and time studies, published as a service for information and implementation.  They  have a great deal of credibility, as they have been scrutinized by industry leaders and are often a result of a financially backed grant that provided adequate time and money for research and development.   Individual institutions must analyze and assess applicability and acceptability of these standards. |
| **Time and Motion** | The "clipboard" and "stopwatch" approach. |

# Logging and Documenting Activities

It is as important to spend time determining the time values as these values reflect the quality commitments for patient services. As much as 90 percent of a nursing department's budget expense is devoted to personnel salaries. That expense directly relates to the labor time it takes to get the work accomplished. Thus, the time standards become the basis of the department's budget activities and productivity system, and the quality commitments target the desired level of care.

**Activity Time Log,** Form 1.1, is an excellent and inexpensive tool that can be used to determine departmental standards. Ideally, each nursing department would have an objective, computerized patient classification system that would provide reliable, valid data for use in developing standards. Because that is not always the reality, other alternatives must be considered that are affordable in terms of both nursing time involvement and dollars.

The logging method is simple. The nurse notes on a log sheet, such as Form 1.1, the length of time it takes to complete a designated activity. Logs can be done on all unit activities or on just one. The length of time an activity is studied depends on how quickly trends are identified. Once a trend is identified (with data to back it up) there's no need to continuelogging it. Later, if the activity changes or if the time doesn't fit, the individual activity can be logged again for a "zoom in" look at how the staff's time is being spent. Some pros and cons on the logging technique for determining the department standard are outlined below.

---

# Using Logging to Determine the Department Standard

- Provides a log sheet of work performed
- Records volume of work completed
- Displays activities and time values

**PRO:** Requires minimal training
Accounts for all time
Provides ongoing control
Applies to nonroutine duties
Most readily accepted by staff
Logs individual productivity

**CON:** Employee disruption
Time consuming
Inconsistency in terminology
Recording exaggerations and errors

---

## Activity Time Log
### Assigning Time Values to Patient Care Activities

Date: _____

| Activity | Staff Instructions: Each time an activity is peformed, 1) write how many minutes it took to complete it in the next open box and 2) initial. | | | | | | | | | | | | | |
|---|---|---|---|---|---|---|---|---|---|---|---|---|---|---|
| | | | | | | | | | | | | | | |
| | | | | | | | | | | | | | | |
| | | | | | | | | | | | | | | |
| | | | | | | | | | | | | | | |
| | | | | | | | | | | | | | | |
| | | | | | | | | | | | | | | |

Using this format to identify and validate time values can be economical, accurate, and informative. It can involve the staff, relying on it's expertise, not only to note how long an activity takes to accomplish but also to sort through activities that are done simultaneously or in conjunction with each other.

### Benefits:

- Average or "most frequently used" times can be assigned to activities.
- Activities and their times accumulate in classification categories so that time values can be totaled and assigned to the category overall.
- Staff who document fast times and demonstrate high-quality work also can be tapped as resources to write those procedures and orient new staff.
- Staff with slow times can be assisted in streamlining their work patterns.
- Staff can document all their activities for a given period, or the unit can collectively work on an "activity of the day."

| Activity | Example Instructions: Each time an activity is peformed, 1) write how many minutes it took to complete it in the next open box and 2) initial. | | | | | | | | | | | | | |
|---|---|---|---|---|---|---|---|---|---|---|---|---|---|---|
| **Patient Bath** | 10 rk | 20 rk | 30 cr | 30 cr | 10 rk | 15 rk | 20 ns | 30 cr | 20 ns | 30 cr | 15 rk | 15 ns | 20 an | 15 rk |
| Blood Pressure | | | | | | | | | | | | | | |
| Admission | | | | | | | | | | | | | | |

1. 280 Total Minutes ÷ 14 activities = 20 minutes average per activity, however, only 4 of 14 actually took that time.

2. Worker "cr" consistently took more time to complete the activity, whereas worker "rk" always took less time.

Form 1.1-Example

# Activity Time Log
## Assigning Time Values to Patient Care Activities

Date: _____

| Activity | Staff Instructions: Each time an activity is peformed, 1) write how many minutes it took to complete it in the next open box and 2) initial. | | | | | | | | | | | | | | | | |
|---|---|---|---|---|---|---|---|---|---|---|---|---|---|---|---|---|---|
| | | | | | | | | | | | | | | | | | |
| | | | | | | | | | | | | | | | | | |
| | | | | | | | | | | | | | | | | | |
| | | | | | | | | | | | | | | | | | |
| | | | | | | | | | | | | | | | | | |
| | | | | | | | | | | | | | | | | | |
| | | | | | | | | | | | | | | | | | |
| | | | | | | | | | | | | | | | | | |
| | | | | | | | | | | | | | | | | | |
| | | | | | | | | | | | | | | | | | |
| | | | | | | | | | | | | | | | | | |
| | | | | | | | | | | | | | | | | | |
| | | | | | | | | | | | | | | | | | |
| | | | | | | | | | | | | | | | | | |
| | | | | | | | | | | | | | | | | | |
| | | | | | | | | | | | | | | | | | |
| | | | | | | | | | | | | | | | | | |
| | | | | | | | | | | | | | | | | | |
| | | | | | | | | | | | | | | | | | |
| | | | | | | | | | | | | | | | | | |

# How Nursing Care Can Benefit
# from the Service Unit

- Quality is protected by a predetermined, prioritized level
  of patient care by individual service units.  Each unit has:

    - Verifiable standards of care as quality targets.

    - Measurable targets identifying the amount of time
      it takes to meet the standards.

    - A role in the nursing care plan; i.e., a group of timed
      activities that when totaled will identify the patient's
      overall labor hour requirement per patient day and
      according to their acuity level.

- Productivity methods can build on service units which:

    - Define patient care activities
        - At a prestated level of quality.
        - In terms of time, providing measurable targets for
            - planning future patient care needs.
            - monitoring and evaluating productivity.

    - Help separate activities and rank in order of priority.
        - Do we really need the service or activity?
        - Do we still want to provide it?

    - Break out the cost-benefit equation.
        - Cost: of professionally skilled labor
        - Benefit: of quality patient care

# Section 2

# Using Nursing Care Standards for Budget Planning

## Ensuring the Preselected Levels of Quality

The best way to ensure a desired level of quality to every patient on every day of their stay is to do it on a unit of service basis whereby there is a standard amount of nursing care hours provided per a 24-hour patient day. Fortunately, the majority of nursing departments already have a Patient Classification System in response to a JCAH (Joint Commission on Accreditation of Hospitals) nursing standard. These systems provide a methodology for determining patient nursing care requirements, and with the addition of time values to each of the classification categories, the classification system can also become a methodology for other very important activities. In this section, patient classification data are used to develop standard hours per patient day (HPPD) that can be used as part of an overall quality and productivity system for delivering patient care.

## What's a Class II?

The usefulness of the classification system increases when time values are added to the classification categories. Although the systems are not all ideal, the majority of nursing departments do have a routine methodology for assigning a patient to a particular classification level, and thus part of the work is already completed. Some nursing departments are fortunate enough to have a time-based, objective, computerized system that generates hours of care needed; others have subjective, manual systems. For this discussion, let's assume that the time value process will be done manually, using the **logging** methodology described in Section 1. Because there are many supplementary materials on patient classification systems, the systems themselves are not discussed here. Rather, the focus is on those activities that can build on a solid classification system to the benefit of both quality and productivity.

# Patient Classification Systems

## JCAH Standard:

To define, implement, and maintain a system for determining patient requirements for nursing care on the basis of demonstrated patient needs, appropriate nursing intervention, and priority for care.

## Additional Applications:

Analysis of cumulative data can be used to develop **standard** nursing care hours per patient day (HPPD). The standard HPPD can be used as:

- The budget target per unit of service to ensure sufficient FTEs to meet both volume and acuity needs.

- Productivity monitors: feed forward, concurrent, and retrospective.

- A key to identifying the cost of nursing care for budgeting expenses, pricing, and price control.

Patients change in acuity and move up or down the classification scale because of (a) the number of nursing activities or (b) the intensity of nursing activities. Nurses are in the best position to identify how much time is involved in those activities and to add up the sum total of the collective activities in a classification category. As a patient's hours are totaled, the classification assignment is made to accommodate any changes in the patient's condition and to determine the number of nursing care hours the patient will need. The time value component can tell how many staff are needed and when to add or delete the next 8-hour staff member to the unit assignment roster.

Thus, if the typical activities for a class I patient are (1) tested for time, (2) totaled, and (3) averaged, one could identify the average hours required for a class I patient. Another approach would be to add up the hours it takes to accomplish a nursing care plan for a group of class I patients and average those hours. Still one other way that may be more popular in the cost-constrained days ahead might be to say, "We have only 3.0 direct nursing care hours available for the class I patient; what are the priority activities that must be accomplished within that constraint?"

There are a number of ways to identify the hours of nursing care needed for the patients on the average, and there will be many more proposed in the future, ranging from time values being assigned to care plans to time values being assigned to standards of care. Each institution must decide its own best way, given its individual situation. In all cases, however, the standard unit of service **must be credible, reliable, and approved for budgetary purposes**. Even the computerized calculations and the consultant's developed standard should be logged and audited periodically, as priorities of care and procedural practices of delivering services are affected by our changing environment.

## Using Classification Data to Validate Standard HPPD

For the remainder of the section let's assume that the time values placed on the individual classification categories are valid. How can this information be useful as a management tool and mechanism for ensuring the designated level of quality per unit of service, in this case, the patient day.

Forms 2.1, 2.2 and 2.3 are essentially variations of the same form, **Calculating Standards Using Retrospective Classification Data**, and in each case the number of patient days, cases, or modalities is counted and weighted to determine how many labor hours are needed to provide the care overall and then on a per patient day, per case, and per modality basis. Patient days, DRG cases, and modalities are used in order to show the versatility of the form for different units of service and also to demonstrate that all nurses are basically doing the same thing. Nursing has a real edge because the patient classification system has been in place for several years and is routinely used.

## Calculating Direct Nursing Care Hours Per Patient Day

Form 2.1-Example, on the following page, simply addresses individual patient days by classification category to derive an average hourly requirement per patient day on the average. Classification categories are weighted so that the sicker, more acutely ill patients who require more nursing care hours accrue more of those hours in the calculations. Although separating patient days into categories works well on paper, patients can't be separated out into neat little categories. Thus, identifying the average care hours needed per patient day leaves the manager in the best position to adjust up or down (due to acuity or volume) on a shift-by-shift basis if units were staffed, in this case, according to the 4.7 HPPD. And the best part of all is that the quality is protected within the identified confines of that 4.7 hours so that it can be guaranteed on the average to every patient, every day.

# Calculating Standards
## Using Retrospective Classification Data

| Classification Category | Patient Days | | Classification Hours Required per Patient Day | | Staff Hours Required |
|---|---|---|---|---|---|
| Classification I | 1,800 | X | 3.0 | = | 5,400 |
| Classification II | 5,000 | X | 4.5 | = | 22,500 |
| Classification III | 2,000 | X | 6.0 | = | 12,000 |
| Classification IV | 400 | X | 8.0 | = | 3,200 |
| Classification V | 0 | X | 12.0 | = | 0 |
| Classification VI | 0 | X | 24.0 | = | 0 |
| Totals | 9,200 | | | | 43,100 |

| Required Hours | ÷ | Patient Days | = | Average Required Nursing Care Hours per Patient Day Based on <u>Acuity</u> and <u>Volume</u> |
|---|---|---|---|---|

| 43,100 | ÷ | 9,200 | = | 4.7 Hours per Patient Day |
|---|---|---|---|---|

<u>Classification hours required per patient day</u> can be derived from one of the methods described in the section Determining Standards, or from a current classification system, if one is in place and adequately describes time allocation per classification category.

This form may be used for any time period of any length, from one day to years, as the calculations are based on patient days and their corresponding required manhours, not length of time.

<u>Patient days</u> can be extracted from department logs or the business office because a room charge is posted daily and accrues as patient days are billed.

Form 2.1 - Example

# Calculating Standards
# Using Retrospective Classification Data

| Classification Category | Patient Days | | Classification Hours Required per Patient Day | | Staff Hours Required |
|---|---|---|---|---|---|
| Classification I | _____ | X | _____ | = | _____ |
| Classification II | _____ | X | _____ | = | _____ |
| Classification III | _____ | X | _____ | = | _____ |
| Classification IV | _____ | X | _____ | = | _____ |
| Classification V | _____ | X | _____ | = | _____ |
| Classification VI | _____ | X | _____ | = | _____ |
| **Totals** | ========= | | | | ========= |

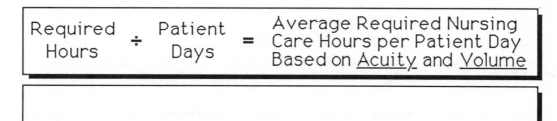

| Required Hours | ÷ | Patient Days | = | Average Required Nursing Care Hours per Patient Day Based on <u>Acuity</u> and <u>Volume</u> |
|---|---|---|---|---|
| _____ | ÷ | _____ | = | _____ |

---

<u>Classification hours required per patient day</u> can be derived from one of the methods described in the section Determining Standards, or from a current classification system, if one is in place and adequately describes time allocation per classification category.

This form may be used for any time period of any length, from one day to years, as the calculations are based on patient days and their corresponding required manhours, not length of time.

<u>Patient days</u> can be extracted from department logs or the business office because a room charge is posted daily and accrues as patient days are billed.

## Calculating Direct Nursing Care Hours per DRG Case

The patient classification categories, when weighted for time, can do exactly the same for DRG categories as with patient days; that is identify an average nursing care requirement per case. The chart below is used for recording classification information for a group of 10 patients who were all in the same DRG category. During each day of their stay the hours required per their classification category were recorded so that average hours per case or per patient day could be calculated. In most nursing units 75 to 80% of the patients fall into 10 or less DRG categories, and even if just those 5 to 10 DRG categories were tracked, there would be sufficient information to budget according to DRG category and determine nursing's part of the DRG pie. Form 2.2-Example, on the following page, shows annual calculations to determine the average nursing care hours per patient day, based on the already calculated average nursing care hours per DRG category.

| Case Number | Total LOS | HOURS REQUIRED EACH INPATIENT DAY – AS PER CLASS* | | | | | | | | | Total Hours |
|---|---|---|---|---|---|---|---|---|---|---|---|
| Case #1 | 8 | 6 | 6 | 6 | 5 | 5 | 4 | 4 | 5 | | 41 |
| Case #2 | 6 | 6 | 6 | 5 | 5 | 4 | 5 | | | | 31 |
| Case #3 | 4 | 6 | 5 | 4 | 5 | | | | | | 20 |
| Case #4 | 9 | 6 | 6 | 6 | 6 | 6 | 6 | 5 | 4 | 5 | 50 |
| Case #5 | 6 | 6 | 6 | 6 | 5 | 5 | 5 | | | | 33 |
| Case #6 | 6 | 6 | 6 | 6 | 5 | 4 | 5 | | | | 32 |
| Case #7 | 7 | 6 | 6 | 6 | 6 | 5 | 4 | 5 | | | 38 |
| Case #8 | 5 | 6 | 6 | 6 | 4 | 5 | | | | | 27 |
| Case #9 | 3 | 5 | 4 | 5 | | | | | | | 14 |
| Case #10 | 6 | 6 | 6 | 6 | 5 | 4 | 5 | | | | 32 |
| PD's | 60 | | | | | | TOTAL REQ'D HOURS = 318 | | | | |

* Assuming that each patient classified as a Class I requires 4.0 nursing care hours per patient day (HPPD) on the average, a class II requires 5.0 HPPD and a class III requires 6.0 HPPD.

# Calculating Standards
# Using Retrospective Classification Data

| DRG Classification Category | Patient Days (ALOS x Adm)* | | Classification Hours Required per Patient Day | | Staff Hours Required |
|---|---|---|---|---|---|
| DRG #23 | 2500 | X | 6.0 | = | 15,000 |
| DRG #104 | 2000 | X | 4.2 | = | 8,400 |
| DRG #110 | 1000 | X | 5.5 | = | 5,500 |
| DRG #235 | 1500 | X | 5.3 | = | 7,950 |
| DRG #300 | 700 | X | 4.8 | = | 3,360 |
| DRG #422 | 300 | X | 5.7 | = | 1,710 |
| **Totals** | 8000 | | | | 41,920 |

| Required Hours | ÷ | Patient Days | = | Average Required Nursing Care Hours per Patient Day Based on <u>Acuity</u> and <u>Volume</u> |
|---|---|---|---|---|

| 41,920 | ÷ | 8000 | = | 5.24 HPPD |
|---|---|---|---|---|

\* Patient Days can be the actual count of days from the business office's days billed, or if those days aren't broken down by DRG, this formula can be used:

(DRG #_____ Average Length of Stay) X ( #_____ Admissions to DRG #_____)

Form 2.2 – Example

# Calculating Standards
# Using Retrospective Classification Data

| DRG Classification Category | Patient Days (ALOS x Adm) | Classification Hours Required per Patient Day | Staff Hours Required |
|---|---|---|---|
| DRG # _____ | _____ | × _____ | = _____ |
| DRG # _____ | _____ | × _____ | = _____ |
| DRG # _____ | _____ | × _____ | = _____ |
| DRG # _____ | _____ | × _____ | = _____ |
| DRG # _____ | _____ | × _____ | = _____ |
| DRG # _____ | _____ | × _____ | = _____ |
| **Totals** | _____ | | _____ |

| Required Hours | ÷ | Patient Days | = | Average Required Nursing Care Hours per Patient Day Based on <u>Acuity</u> and <u>Volume</u> |
|---|---|---|---|---|

_____ ÷ _____ = _____

### Calculating Direct Nursing Care Hours per Patient Modality

Although the discussion in this workbook is directed toward the inpatient patient day, some diversion to outpatient activities is irresistible, especially when the process and outcome are so dramatically similar. Nursing is becoming more and more involved in activities other than inpatient nursing, including home health visits, emergency department nursing charges, triaging interventions, outpatient nursing, prevention, health promotion, education, and the likes. In the past, because there was no methodology set up for charging for these services, they were more than occasionally done for free. Nursing has been at the forefront of some of the new entrepreneurial ventures that catapult them out of the inpatient arena and into modality-based charging.

Thus, Form 2.3-Example, on the next page, demonstrates the identical process used with inpatient nursing, but with time values assigned to the individual modalities to weight them for nursing care intensity and time involvement. Once again, the individual time values, as well as the overall .72 hours per modality (43 minutes), can be used for budget planning and control and can become the basis of the productivity system.

---

## The present is a time of great entrepreneurial ferment, where old and staid institutions suddenly have to become very limber.

- Peter Drucker

---

# Calculating Standards
# Using Retrospective Classification Data

| Department Modalities | Modalities Completed & Charged | | Hours Required per Modality | | Staff Hours Required |
|---|---|---|---|---|---|
| Modality #1 | 5,000 | X | 0.5 | = | 2,500 |
| Modality #2 | 7,000 | X | 0.75 | = | 5,250 |
| Modality #3 | 1,000 | X | 1.0 | = | 1,000 |
| Modality #4 | 600 | X | 1.25 | = | 750 |
| Modality #5 | 300 | X | 1.5 | = | 450 |
| Modality #6 | 100 | X | 1.75 | = | 175 |
| Totals | 14,000 | | | | 10,125 |

| Total Required Hours | ÷ | Total Modalities | = | Average Required Direct Care Hours per Modality Based on Acuity & Volume |
|---|---|---|---|---|

$$10,125 \div 14,000 = .72 \text{ Hours (43 minutes)}$$

Hours required per modality can be derived from one of the methods described in the section, Determining Standards, or from an existing classification system if one is in place and accurately identifies time allocation per modality.

This form may be used for any period of any length, from one day to years, as the calculations are based on modalities and their corresponding required manhours, not length of time.

Modalities can be extracted from department logs or the business office because a charge is posted each time a modality is completed.

Form 2.3 – Example

## Calculating Standards
## Using Retrospective Classification Data

| Department Modalities | Modalities Completed & Charged | | Hours Required per Modality | | Staff Hours Required |
|---|---|---|---|---|---|
| Modality #1 | | × | | = | |
| Modality #2 | | × | | = | |
| Modality #3 | | × | | = | |
| Modality #4 | | × | | = | |
| Modality #5 | | × | | = | |
| Modality #6 | | × | | = | |
| **Totals** | | | | | |

| Total Required Hours | ÷ | Total Modalities | = | Average Required Direct Care Hours per Modality Based on Acuity & Volume |
|---|---|---|---|---|
| _____ | ÷ | _____ | = | _____ |

Hours required per modality can be derived from one of the methods described in the section, Determining Standards, or from an existing classification system if one is in place and accurately identifies time allocation per modality.

This form may be used for any period of any length, from one day to years, as the calculations are based on modalities and their corresponding required manhours, not length of time.

Modalities can be extracted from department logs or the business office because a charge is posted each time a modality is completed.

# What if the Calculated Standard is Not Approved?

Another reason for identifying the activities and time values for the activities within each classification category is to assist the staff nurse and nurse manager in making decisions about the priorities of care for the patient. With lengths of stay shortening, the patients who remain in the hospital are sicker, and have higher acuities and more nursing care needs. At the same time, nurse managers with excellent documentation from their classification systems for increased staff may be turned down for additional FTEs because the need is not due to an increase in volume of patient days and the revenue attached to those days is not increasing. Budget committees have already responded with statements indicating that they are aware that the patients are sicker, but the money is not available to pay for additional hours. Although these issues are not dealt with specifically until the third workbook of this series, it is useful information that helps the nurse manager look and plan ahead during budget planning and calculation phases.

Solutions that once seemed impractical are now being considered. One alternative being considered by many organizations is to charge patients for nursing care according to their acuity level. This option has two advantages. One, it is fairest to all levels of patients, and two, when the patient needs more care there is the capability to increase care according to classified needs and to accrue the revenue to enable the purchase of additional labor hours as needed.

Another option is to go back and rework the classification categories, taking out activities that can be accomplished by a family member or another department. But the average classified HPPD may still be more than the budget can afford. If this is the case, activities should be looked at again and prioritized according to standards of care and patient care goals so that the lowest priority activities can be designated as a "when time permits" activity. A classification system that continually calls for more care hours than are available or approved will create frustration for the staff and eventually will be viewed as a meaningless exercise, rather than one of the most significant patient care management tools available.

# Section 3

# Using the Nursing Care Standard for Budget Calculation

## The Budget Process

Many managers incorrectly think that the budget is an allowance. In reality it is an ongoing process of planning for the upcoming fiscal year. The primary goal for a department is to deliver a particular level of quality services to the patient. That quality is defined by both the standards of care and the unit of service, which describes how much time it takes in labor hours to deliver that level of quality. Thus funding is needed to hire sufficient personnel to provide "X" labor hours per patient day ( HPPD) but no more than "X", and that's where it gets tricky.

Budgeting and managing productivity become easy tasks once the unit of service is developed and approved. The process begins by planning for "X" HPPD for every patient day expected in the new fiscal year and ends with building the rest of the budget around it, theoretically protecting it (this will be clearer after reading through the examples). For the purpose of this section, 3.0 HPPD is used as the unit standard.[1]

---

## The budget is a plan...not an allowance. If the approving body likes the plan then they approve the funds to put the plan into action.

---

[1] Although the example addresses only patient days that accrue from inpatient room charges, the theory in this section and Form 2.4 are set up to accommodate "modality" volume as well. Home health and out-patient endeavors accrue visits, tests, procedures, etc., and these are all defined as modalities.

## Calculating the FTE[2]
## Required to Deliver the Desired Level of Quality

Once the unit of service is established and validated, it can be used as the focal point of all personnel budgetary planning. And although it is true that "numbers" are now directing the plans for patient care, one must remember that they are based on standards of care that identify the preselected level of quality.

In the next sections the flexible (or variable, as is it sometimes called) budget process is followed from the initial step of determining direct care manhours through the final outcome of total FTEs for the new fiscal year. Flexible budgeting is an easy process to learn if taken one step at a time; thus the process is described in several sections. Taken together, they comprise the body of Form 2.4. The graphs below demonstrate the difference between (1) a fixed budget system where staffing remains constant regardless of variations in census, (2) a completely flexible system that increases and decreases staffing solely on the basis of volume, and (3) the most frequently used in health care, a semi-flexible system that has about 12 to15% fixed (those staff members who do not increase and decrease according to volume, such as clinicians, clerks, managers, etc.) with the remaining staff as flexible and volume adjusted. The last system is the one that is used for the example.

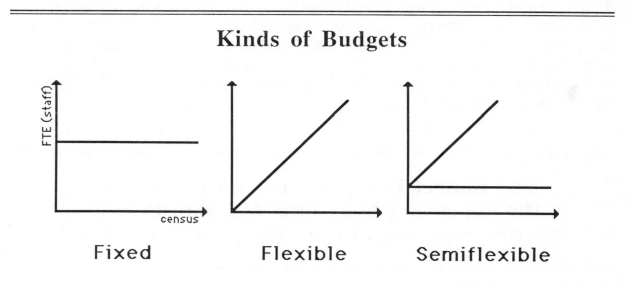

# Kinds of Budgets

Fixed　　　　Flexible　　　Semiflexible

---

[2] a Full-time equivalent (FTE) is a position for a full time employee or two or more part time employees. It is equal to 2080 hours annually, so if an employee works 40 hours a week for the entire year, they have filled the position. If that employee cuts their working hours to 24 hours a week (3 days), then another part time person can be hired to work the other 16 hours (2 days) each week. For budgetary purposes the FTE (the positions) are approved not the individual employees. A chart describing different ways an FTE can be split is at the end of the section.

# Volume

The first step in determining how many staff members you need for the new fiscal year (FY) is to predict, as closely as possible, what the volume or activity level will be in the new year. Is the service growing, shrinking, remaining constant? Historical data, market research and communication with purchasers of health care (patients, physicians, third party payers, HMOs, PPOs, etc.) all provide information that will help support the guess. Every conceivable statistical, analytical, and computerized system has been used over the years to forecast volume (some financial wizards have been known to hide crystal balls under their desks), but there is always a variance between what is anticipated and what is real. Using the HPPD approach enables the nurse manager to adjust to any volume on any shift and maintain the budget goal throughout the fiscal year.

## Volume:   patient days accrued year-to-date or a projection of future demand

The volume in the example below is forecasted to grow 10% annually in the next fiscal year. Therefore, a 10% growth factor is used to accumulate mathematically the anticipated increase in patient day volume.

**PROJECTION OF PATIENT DAYS FOR NEW FISCAL YEAR (FY)**

1.  $\dfrac{\text{10,000}}{\substack{\text{Actual Patient Days or} \\ \text{Modalities for the Last} \\ \text{12 Months}}}$  **X**  $\dfrac{\text{.10}}{\substack{\text{Projected Growth} \\ \text{Factor of a} \\ \text{Preselected Percent}}}$  **=**  $\dfrac{\text{1,000}}{\substack{\text{Projected Increase in the} \\ \text{Number of Patient Days or} \\ \text{Modalities for the New FY}}}$

2.  $\dfrac{\text{10,000}}{\substack{\text{Actual Patient Days or} \\ \text{Modalities for the last} \\ \text{12 months}}}$  **+**  $\dfrac{\text{1,000}}{\substack{\text{Projected increase} \\ \text{in Number of Patient} \\ \text{Days or Modalities}}}$  **=**  $\dfrac{\text{11,000}}{\substack{\text{Projected \textbf{Total Patient}} \\ \textbf{Days or Modalities} \text{ for} \\ \text{the New Fiscal Year}}}$

# Flexible (Direct) FTE

Historically, even the best guesses miss the mark, and that's part of the beauty of a flexible budget. Because it is volume-based ("X" HPPD) the manager needs only provide the unit standard, 3.0 HPPD in this case, for each of the patient days anticipated. The next step, #4, is to divide the large number of hours by the number of hours a full-time equivalent (hereafter, FTE) works annually, 2080 hours, to ascertain how many full-time positions are needed to deliver the direct aspect of care to the patient.

Flexible (direct) FTEs refer only to the FTEs devoted to hands-on care of the patients. In the semiflexible budget illustration on page 26, the diagonal line demonstrates the action of volume-based adjustments that increase and decrease staff to match increases and decreases in volume. In step #3 of the example below, 15.9 FTEs need to be hired just to guarantee every patient 3 hours of direct care every day on the average; if the volume doubled to 22,000 projected days, the number of FTEs would also double because the goal remains the same, providing each patient 3.0 labor hours of care each day of their stay, on the average.

**CALCULATION OF FLEXIBLE (DIRECT) FTES: BASED ON UNIT STANDARD**

3.
| 3.0 | | 11,000 | | 33,000 |
|---|---|---|---|---|
| UNIT STANDARD: Flexible (Direct) Hours of Care Per Patient Day or per Modality | X | Projected Total Patient Days or Modalities for New Fiscal Year | = | Total Flexible (Direct) Manhours Required for the New Fiscal Year |

4.
| 33,000 | | 2080 | | 15.9 |
|---|---|---|---|---|
| Total Flexible (Direct) Manhours Required | ÷ | Hours Worked Annually per FTE (Full-Time Equivalent) | = | Total Flexible (Direct) FTEs |

Naturally, not every patient on a unit receives exactly the same amount of direct care on a daily basis. Such factors as acuity, physician orders, and patient and family expectations and personalities all play a part in how much time a nurse spends with a particular patient. It's important to keep good records of classification data so that the average HPPD can be continually validated and updated for accuracy.

# Fixed FTE

All labor hours are not volume related. Indirect care, such as work done by secretaries, clerks, managers or clinicians, for example, is not directly affected by the volume or acuity level of the patients on the unit and may continue to increase even when the census decreases. The work of the manager, for example, can increase when the census declines and staff members need to be reallocated or called off. In addition, clinicians have some of their best opportunities for inservice education at those times. Over the long run, however, their work should decline proportionately with the volume of patient days even though it is not directly related to the patient day and is not flexible.

Careful planning is needed for allocating fixed FTE hours because fixed costs can be very expensive, particularly if the census declines and hours are not reduced proportionately within a reasonable time or without an approved reason. As step #5 shows, the 3.0 total fixed FTE are simply added to the flexible (direct) FTEs with no specific relationship to the number of those FTEs or the projected volume (although 10 to 15 percent is usually acceptable). Because they are not volume related, fixed positions require a good deal of justification.

---

**FIXED FTES**

5.  **15.9**                +      **3.0** { 1.0 Manager }    =    **18.9**
    Total Flexible                     { 2.0 Clerks }         Total Productive FTEs
    (Direct) FTEs                 **Total Fixed FTEs**          (Worked Hours)

---

In the example above, the manager is budgeted at 1.0 fixed. That means that there are sufficient hours for the manager to spend all of the full-time working hours, 40 hours a week, on management activities without affecting direct patient care. Other managers are not so lucky, and in fact, when they work this 7-step series backwards for their units, they discover that their hours are flexible, not fixed. When this is the case, the manager either is tied to direct patient care, or if the manager does indirect work, the available hours of care to the patient are reduced and the preplanned 3.0 hours of care may fall to 2.7.

Managers should assess how much management work needs to be done and budget those hours as fixed (even if it's only 1 day a week, i.e. .2 FTE). Then they'll be able to take on additional responsibilities and be held accountable for results.

# Nonproductive FTE

The last group of hours to consider are those of the Nonproductive FTEs, the full-time equivalents required for the sole purpose of covering the direct care FTEs when they are using paid benefit time, i.e. being paid but not working. Paid time off for vacation, holiday, jury duty, death leave, sickness, etc. is now the norm. Full-time employees may be off-duty with full pay for a minimum of 3 weeks annually, and if the time is provided without giving consideration to coverage for those absent employees, the HPPD and standards of care would be directly and dramatically affected. Thus, it is good planning to look ahead, identify the average benefit hours to be paid to the staff members in the particular department, and calculate how many hours they'll be away and have to be replaced if the anticipated census becomes a reality.

In step #6 each staff member, on the average, earns and takes 15 vacation days of 8 hours each, 8 holiday days, and 32 hours of sick time as based on the prior year's averages. The total, 216 hours for each of the 18.9 FTEs adds up to enough hours, 4082 annually, to hire the equivalent of two FTEs just to cover the 18.9 FTEs when they are on paid leave from the institution.

---

**NONPRODUCTIVE FTES**

6.  $\underset{\text{Total Productive FTEs}}{18.9}$  X  $216 \left\{ \begin{array}{l} \text{15 vac, 8 holiday} \\ \text{4 sick} \times \text{8 hours} \end{array} \right\}$ $\underset{\text{Worked per each FTE}}{\underset{\text{Hours for Hours Not}}{\text{Nonproductive Paid}}}$  =  $\underset{\substack{\text{Hours Required to Cover} \\ \text{Nonproductive Paid Time.} \\ \text{(Divide by 2080 for FTEs)}}}{4082 \div 2080 = 2.0}$

Note: If fixed FTEs are not replaced when they use benefit time, exclude them from this calculation and use flexible (direct) FTEs only.

---

The resulting 2.0 nonproductive FTEs in the calculation above might create the impression that two full-time employees should be hired to cover vacations, holidays, etc. Every effort should be made to resist that temptation and to use part-time and per diem staff to (1) increase the number of people available to cover and (2) to provide as much flexibility as possible in being able to grant staff members more than two benefit days at a time.

# Total Adjusted FTE

The sum total of flexible (direct), fixed and nonproductive FTEs is the total adjusted FTEs, which is called "adjusted" because adjustments were made to fixed and nonproductive hours to enable the actual provision of the 3.0 HPPD of care to the patients.   The total adjusted FTE figure becomes the next fiscal year's position control; that is, the number of FTEs that can be hired.  The position control remains constant for the remainder of that fiscal year unless there is an approved adjustment by the budget committee, and in today's environment most of the approved adjustments are strictly for increases in patient day volume that have already occurred.  However, because this is a flexible budget, flexibility has been built in so that on a shift-by-shift basis if the census is up or down, staffing can be adjusted based on providing 3.0 HPPD to every patient every day.

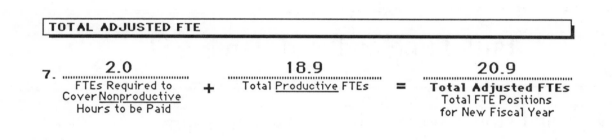

TOTAL ADJUSTED FTE

7.
$$\underset{\substack{\text{FTEs Required to} \\ \text{Cover } \underline{\text{Nonproductive}} \\ \text{Hours to be Paid}}}{2.0} + \underset{\text{Total } \underline{\text{Productive}} \text{ FTEs}}{18.9} = \underset{\substack{\textbf{Total Adjusted FTEs} \\ \text{Total FTE Positions} \\ \text{for New Fiscal Year}}}{20.9}$$

# Adjusted Care Hours Per Patient Day (HPPD)

Working backward from the 20.9 total adjusted FTE result on the next page shows that, in order to guarantee 3.0 HPPD  for direct patient care, the institution must pay for 4.0 hours of labor time.   Direct care accounts for 3.0 hours of the labor expense, and the 1.0 additional hour covers overhead expenses of fixed FTE hours and paid benefit time.  In some institutions, the only data available to the nurse manager are the total adjusted FTEs.  Calculating step # 8 tells the total adjusted hours, and calculating steps #1-7 backwards leads to the hours that are available to the patient for direct care.  The importance of the nurse manager knowing the available direct care hours for a particular unit is critical because without that information quality standards and productivity targets cannot be set or worked toward by the staff.

```
┌─────────────────────────────────────────────────────────────┐
│ TOTAL ADJUSTED CARE HOURS PER PATIENT DAY (HPPD)              │
└─────────────────────────────────────────────────────────────┘
```

8.  **20.9**          **2080**          **43472**          **11,000**          **4.0**
    Total             Annual            Adjusted           Projected Total      **Adjusted**
    Adjusted    X     Hours Paid   =    Manhours     ÷     Patient Days or  =   HPPD or per
    FTEs              per FTE           Required           Modalities (#2)      Modality

Note (#2):  Refer to Step #2 for the projected total patient days or modalities.

# Full-Time and Part-Time FTEs

| Days and Hours Worked in a 2-Week Period | Annual Hours | % of 1.0 FTE |
|---|---|---|
| 80 hours ....10 days | 2080 | 1.0 |
| 64 hours .... 8 days | 1664 | .8 |
| 48 hours .... 6 days | 1248 | .6 |
| 40 hours .... 5 days | 1040 | .5 |
| 32 hours .... 4 days* | 832 | .4 |
| 16 hours .... 2 days | 416 | .2 |

* Standard relief for a 7-day per week position. The 1.0 FTE works 5 days, and the .4 works the other 2 days.

# Budget Calculation Form

## PROJECTION OF PATIENT DAYS FOR NEW FISCAL YEAR (FY)

1. **10,000**
Actual Patient Days or Modalities for the Last 12 Months

X **.10**
Projected Growth Factor of a Preselected Percent

= **1,000**
Projected Increase in the Number of Patient Days or Modalities for the New FY

2. **10,000**
Actual Patient Days or Modalities for the last 12 months

+ **1,000**
Projected increase in Number of Patient Days or Modalities

= **11,000**
Projected **Total Patient Days or Modalities** for the New Fiscal Year

## CALCULATION OF FLEXIBLE (DIRECT) FTES: BASED ON UNIT STANDARD

3. **3.0**
UNIT STANDARD: Flexible (Direct) Hours of Care Per Patient Day or per Modality

X **11,000**
Projected Total Patient Days or Modalities for New Fiscal Year

= **33,000**
**Total Flexible (Direct) Manhours** Required for the New Fiscal Year

4. **33,000**
Total Flexible (Direct) Manhours Required

÷ **2080**
Hours Worked Annually per FTE (Full-Time Equivalent)

= **15.9**
**Total Flexible (Direct) FTEs**

## FIXED FTES

5. **15.9**
Total Flexible (Direct) FTEs

+ **3.0** {1.0 Manager, 2.0 Clerks}
**Total Fixed FTEs**

= **18.9**
**Total Productive FTEs** (Worked Hours)

## NONPRODUCTIVE FTES

6. **18.9**
Total Productive FTEs

X **216** {15 vac, 8 holiday, 4 sick x 8 hours}
Nonproductive Paid Hours for Hours Not Worked per each FTE

= **4082 ÷ 2080 = 2.0**
Hours Required to Cover Nonproductive Paid Time. (Divide by 2080 for FTEs)

## TOTAL ADJUSTED FTE

7. **2.0**
FTEs Required to Cover Nonproductive Hours to be Paid

+ **18.9**
Total Productive FTEs

= **20.9**
**Total Adjusted FTEs** Total FTE Positions for New Fiscal Year

Form 3.1 - Example

# Budget Calculation Form

## PROJECTION OF PATIENT DAYS FOR NEW FISCAL YEAR (FY)

**1.** Actual Patient Days _or_ Modalities for the Last 12 Months **X** Projected Growth Factor of a Preselected Percent **=** Projected Increase in the Number of Patient Days or Modalities for the New FY

**2.** Actual Patient Days _or_ Modalities for the last 12 months **+** Projected increase in Number of Patient Days _or_ Modalities **=** Projected **Total Patient Days _or_ Modalities** for the New Fiscal Year

## CALCULATION OF FLEXIBLE (DIRECT) FTES: BASED ON UNIT STANDARD

**3.** UNIT STANDARD: Flexible (Direct) Hours of Care Per Patient Day _or_ per Modality **X** Projected Total Patient Days _or_ Modalities for New Fiscal Year **=** **Total Flexible (Direct) Manhours** Required for the New Fiscal Year

**4.** Total Flexible (Direct) Manhours Required **÷** Hours Worked Annually per FTE (Full-Time Equivalent) **=** **Total Flexible (Direct) FTEs**

## FIXED FTES

**5.** Total Flexible (Direct) FTEs **+** **Total Fixed FTEs** **=** **Total Productive FTEs** (Worked Hours)

## NONPRODUCTIVE FTES

**6.** Total Productive FTEs **X** Nonproductive Paid Hours for Hours Not Worked per each FTE **=** Hours Required to Cover Nonproductive Paid Time. (Divide by 2080 for FTEs)

## TOTAL ADJUSTED FTE

**7.** FTEs Required to Cover _Nonproductive_ Hours to be Paid **+** Total _Productive_ FTEs **=** **Total Adjusted FTEs** Total FTE Positions for New Fiscal Year

Form 3.1
page 34

# Section 4

# Staffing Pattern Development

## Using Standard Hours Per Patient Day

Planning is the the most important of the management functions because the other management functions-organizing, staffing, leading, and control-all build on planning.   Goals are central to the entire management process:

- **Planning** defines the goals.
- Institutions are **organized** and **staffed** to achieve the goals.
- **Leadership** stimulates personnel toward accomplishment of goals.
- **Control** compares outcomes with goal targets to evaluate results.

Having the right amount of staff members on duty for a given census of patients with varying levels of acuity is the result of careful planning, not happenstance. With such tight constraints on money, nursing departments can no longer afford overstaffing.  Staffing overages will ultimately result in either reduced profits or intentional understaffing at some future time if budget targets are to be met. In the past when hospitals operated under fixed budget systems, the patients fluctuated instead of the staff.  On the busy days the staff members would work like crazy, and on the slower days (census- or acuity-wise) they recuperated. The patients in the unit on the busy days got far less, in terms of nursing time, than the negotiated unit standard, whereas the patients who happened to be in the unit on the slow days sometimes received the equivalent of ICU care.

However, by determining a unit standard of service, there is (1) guaranteed quality to the patient and (2) a measure of how long it takes to deliver that level of quality, keeping in mind it will take more time as the patient's acuity increases.  The combination of those two goals provides the initial planning steps to offering quality care to patients on a shift by shift, daily basis through the use of the unit **standard** hours per patient day (HPPD).

Once the standard is developed and approved, it can be used as the focal point in the development of a staffing pattern. A staffing pattern is simply the annual scheduling plan designed to accommodate the average census at the average acuity level. When staff members are routinely prescheduled according to such a plan, the manager is in the best possible position to allocate them in order to meet whatever fluctuations in census occur. Variations in patient acuity occur as well as census increases and decreases, so planning for the average creates more flexibility for reallocations when the actual day arrives. Every reader knows that, on days when staffing is short, the census inevitably shoots up with high-acuity patients.

## Preparing Data for the Staffing Pattern

Continuing with the example from the last section, assume once again that the approved unit of service standard is 3.0 HPPD. If, in fact, 11,000 patient days were projected, then the **average daily census** is expected to be 30 patients, on the average (11,000 ÷ 365). The department goal in this case is to ensure 3.0 hours of care, on the average, to each of its 30 patients within a 24-hour period, so that the average required hours-the desired level of quality-can be delivered. Thus, if an average of 30 patients are anticipated, the manager should preschedule 90 labor hours daily (30 patients X 3.0 HPPD), or 11.3 staff working 8-hour shifts.

| | |
|---|---|
| 30.0 | Average daily census |
| x 3.0 | Average direct HPPD |
| 90 | Hours required to staff the unit 24-hours daily |
| ÷ 8 | Hours in a normal work day |
| **11.3** | **Target number of staff to be prescheduled daily** |

For a department that provides care 24-hours a day, some decision must be made regarding the distribution of the workload.  All 3.0 HPPD can't be given on the day shift unless there is some way to put the patients on automatic pilot after 3:00 P.M.  On the other hand if the the 3.0 HPPD were split evenly (1 hour or 33 percent of 3.0 HPPD per shift) then the night shift may have too much staff on a unit where the workload usually diminishes after patients go to sleep.   Thus, each department must make a conscious decision about workload distribution based on (1) the times patient care activities usually take place and (2) the availability of professional resources.  For example, if in an ICU 33 percent of the workload falls on 11-7, but staff members cannot be found to work the shift and they are already rotating,  the workload should be analyzed to see if any part of the work can be redistributed to another shift without reducing the level of quality.  It may only reduce the staffing needs from six nurses to five, but it may also mean one less rotation a month for the day shift.  Conversely, and even on a daily basis, if there is an extra person scheduled on 3-11 and 7-3 is short, maybe some other patient care activities, such as baths, could be left for the afternoon or evening shift.

| SHIFT | % OF WORK LOAD BY SHIFT | DIRECT CARE HOURS PER PT. DAY OR MODAL. | DAILY FTES |
|---|---|---|---|
| 7-3 | 45% | 1.4 | 5.1 |
| 3-11 | 35% | 1.0 | 4.0 |
| 11-7 | 20% | .6 | 2.2 |
| 3-SHIFT TOTAL | 100% | 3.0 | 11.3 * |

* Daily FTEs = ANNUAL PROJECTED PATIENT DAYS  +  WORKING DAYS IN THE YEAR
(365 for units open 7 days per week, 260 for units open 5 days per week)  X   STANDARD  +  8 HOURS

Chart 4.1

In Chart 4.1 above, the department has decided to distribute 45 percent of the workload to 7-3, 35 percent  to 3-11, and 20 percent to nights.  That means that the 3.0 HPPD are also split up by those percentages. On the 7-3 shift each patient, on the average, is given 1.4 hours of care by the RN, LPN, aide or in combination. In a 8-hour shift a nurse can carry a caseload of about six patients $(8 \div 1.4 = \mathbf{5.7})$, giving each an average of 1.4 hours of care on the 7-3 shift.[3]

In addition to splitting up the care hours by the preselected percentages, the daily FTEs, or actual employees assigned onduty on a given day, should also be split according to the same percentages. For example, if a nurse manager wants 45 percent of the care given on 7-3, then 45 percent of the care hours should be allocated to 7-3. In order to be able to staff 45 percent of the daily FTEs on duty to 7-3, 45 percent of the FTE that are hired to provide flexible (direct) care must be assigned to 7-3 also, as shown in Chart 4.2 below.

| SHIFT | FLEXIBLE (DIRECT) FTES | | NON-PRODUCTIVE FTES | | FIXED FTES | | TOTAL FTES |
|---|---|---|---|---|---|---|---|
| 7-3 | 7.2 | + | 1.0 | + | 2.0 | = | 10.2 |
| 3-11 | 5.5 | + | .6 | + | 1.0 | = | 7.1 |
| 11-7 | 3.2 | + | .4 | + | — | = | 3.6 |
| 3-SHIFT TOTAL | 15.9 | | 2.0 | | 3.0 | | 20.9 |

Chart 4.2

The nonproductive FTEs can follow the same percentage rule, but this decision is made at the discretion of the manager and depends on several variables. First, some areas are still experiencing a nursing shortage on some shifts or in some

---

[3] The 3.0 HPPD can also be some combination of RN, LPN, and other caregivers. This is a management decision and would probably be based on the standards of care and activities that fall in the classification categories. Because the goal of this workbook is to teach process, the decision not to break down the care hours for different skill levels was based on keeping the teaching process as simple as possible, and is not a judgment regarding how care should be given.

units. If flexible positions on the 11-7 shift cannot be filled, there's no sense adding more nonproductive FTE slots that will remain vacant. Second, if because of the shortage, the day shift is covering the assigned 11-7 benefit time, it may be preferable to move the 11-7 nonproductive FTEs to the day shift so that at least the day shift staff won't have to work short when co-workers are rotating to cover 11-7.

Flexibility is the key to covering nonproductive hours. Hiring three full-time people to cover the benefit time of 15.9 other staff members limits flexibility and the manager's ability to grant time off, as requested. Most managers agree that benefit time is precious and should be given as requested whenever possible (as opposed to forcing someone to take time off at an undesirable time just because staff is available to cover). Here are a few ways nonproductive hours can be handled to give maximum flexibility to both management and staff. First, several units can combine their nonproductive FTEs to carve out a shared float pool of staff. Second, the FTEs can be used to hire a group of per diem staff, rather than, as in the example above, hiring 3.0 full-timers. Third, if the unit already has a number of part-time staff members who are willing and interested in covering extra shifts, the 3.0 FTEs can be left vacant so that the funds are available to pay the already experienced part-time staff for the extra hours they work.

Finally, fixed FTEs are the exception to the percentage rule. Fixed staff are assigned where they are needed to do their work. If 100 percent are working on the 7-3 shift, that's where their FTEs should be on the staffing pattern and where they will be assigned to work. Thus, the assignment of the 3.0 fixed FTEs above is not related to the direct care distribution. There are a manager and a unit clerk on 7-3 and a unit clerk on 3-11, and their assignments appear on the staffing pattern as such.

Performing all the calculations on the preceding pages may seem a long way around an activity that one may already be accomplishing for the most part through trial and error and sheer luck. However, the additional planning time at the beginning of the fiscal year will pay off in terms of fine tuning the action plan for meeting the budget and productivity targets. By starting out on the right track, staffed on target, it will be much easier to meet the budget and productivity targets and avoid compromising the quality target of 3.0 HPPD.

# Creating the Daily Staffing Pattern

If the work on the preceding pages has been completed properly, creating the staffing pattern should be easy. Looking just at the 7-3 section of the staffing pattern, in Pattern 4.1 below, and taking the information from Chart 3.2, the fixed positions are the easiest to place in the pattern because they are approved for 1.0 FTE each. That means there are enough hours and dollars for the employees in those positions to work 5 days a week, but there's no coverage for their 2 days off each week. That would entail adding another .4 FTE for each of the fixed positions (See Section 3, Fixed FTE).

## 7-3 Shift

| Position | Daily | Total |
|----------|-------|-------|
| Flex: | | |
| Flex: | | |
| Flex: | | |
| Nonprod: | | |
| Fixed: **Manager** | 1.0 | 1.0 |
| Fixed: **Unit Clerk** | 1.0 | 1.0 |
| **Total FTEs 7-3** | | |

Pattern 4.1

In Pattern 4.2, on the following page, the nonproductive FTEs are placed in the pattern. Again, this is fairly simple as the nonproductive FTEs only work when the staff from the daily staffing pattern are using benefit time. Thus, the 1.0 nonproductive FTE should be shown not in the daily column but in its entirety in the total column as it is part of the total FTEs. It is not absolutely crucial to break down the nonproductive positions by skill level in the staffing pattern because they are replacement staff only. In Pattern 4.2 all of the nonproductive FTEs are budgeted for RN level. **Form 4.1 - Example** shows the nonproductive broken down by skill level, and Forms 4.2 and 4.3 are set up to combine all nonproductive positions together, the simplest of the methods.

## 7-3 Shift

| Position | Daily | Total |
|---|---|---|
| Flex: | | |
| Flex: | | |
| Flex: | | |
| Nonprod: **RN** | 0 | 1.0 |
| Fixed: Manager | 1.0 | 1.0 |
| Fixed: Unit Clerk | 1.0 | 1.0 |
| **Total FTEs 7-3** | | |

Pattern 4.2

In the next step below, the flexible FTEs are placed in Pattern 4.3. According to Chart 4.1 there can be a total of 5.1 flexible staff on daily and because they are on 7 days a week, 7.2 flexible (direct) FTEs have been budgeted (5.1 x 1.4 = 7.2 FTE) so that the daily pattern can be achieved.

## 7-3 Shift

| Position | Daily | Total |
|---|---|---|
| Flex: **RN** | 2.0 | 2.8 |
| Flex: **LPN** | 1.0 | 1.4 |
| Flex: **Aide** | 2.1 | 3.0 |
| Nonprod: RN | 0 | 1.0 |
| Fixed: Manager | 1.0 | 1.0 |
| Fixed: Unit Clerk | 1.0 | 1.0 |
| **Total FTEs 7-3** | **5.1** | **7.2** |

Note #1: For every FTE working 7 days a week, 1.0 covers 5 of the days but another .4 is needed to cover the 2 days off of the 1.0 FTE.

Note #2: 5.1 daily in the reality of a schedule means that every day there are five staff scheduled on, but 1 day during a pay period a sixth person could be added without going over budget.

Pattern 4.3

In the final pattern the manager has the opportunity to fine tune and make minor adjustments to the pattern based on how well the pattern fits with the reality of the staffing situation.  For example, in Pattern 4.4 below, the manager has made the decision to upgrade .2 of the LPN FTEs to RN in order to be able to hire three full-time RNs rather than 2.8 RNs.  Although some managers do not feel a .8 position is very attractive for hiring purposes, other managers support the 32-hour work week as a norm for the full-timer because it allows the nursing department 8 hours of straight pay (as opposed to overtime pay)  to use during census increases.

## 7-3 Shift

| Position | Daily | Total |
|---|---|---|
| Flex: RN | 2.0 | **3.0** |
| Flex: LPN | 1.0 | **1.2** |
| Flex: Aide | 2.1 | 3.0 |
| Nonprod: RN | 0 | 1.0 |
| Fixed: Manager | 1.0 | 1.0 |
| Fixed: Unit Clerk | 1.0 | 1.0 |
| **Total FTEs 7-3** | **7.1** | **10.2** |

Pattern 4.4

When the pattern is complete as in **Staffing Pattern,** Form **4.1 - Example,** on the following page, the manager has a format to follow for filling out the time schedules for the remainder of the fiscal year.

The blank forms have been developed and provided in two ways.  **Staffing Pattern,** Form **4.1,** is the same as the example form and **Staffing Pattern,** Form **4.2** is a modified version designed for the final staffing pattern only.  Either one is acceptable.

# Staffing Pattern

Department __North Wing__  Fiscal Year __1986__  Unit of Service __3.0 HPPD__
Flexible FTEs __15.9__ Fixed FTEs __3.0__ Nonproductive __2.0__ Total FTEs __20.9__

## Staffing Pattern Information

| SHIFT | % OF WORK LOAD BY SHIFT | DIRECT CARE HOURS PER PT. DAY OR MODAL. | DAILY FTES | FLEXIBLE (DIRECT) FTES | | NON-PRODUCTIVE FTES | | FIXED FTES | | TOTAL FTES |
|---|---|---|---|---|---|---|---|---|---|---|
| 7-3 | 45% | 1.4 | 5.1 | 7.2 | + | 1.0 | + | 2.0 | = | 10.2 |
| 3-11 | 35% | 1.0 | 4.0 | 5.5 | + | .6 | + | 1.0 | = | 7.1 |
| 11-7 | 20% | .6 | 2.2 | 3.2 | + | .4 | + | — | = | 3.6 |
| 3-SHIFT TOTAL | 100% | 3.0 | 11.3* | 15.9 | | 2.0 | | 3.0 | | 20.9 |

*Patient Days ÷ Work Days in Year (7-day units = 365, 5-day units = 260) X Standard ÷ 8 Hours.

| 7-3 Positions | | Daily | Total |
|---|---|---|---|
| Flex: | RN | 2.0 | 2.8 |
| Flex: | LPN | 1.0 | 1.4 |
| Flex: | Aide | 2.1 | 3.0 |
| Nonprod: | RN | 0 | 1.0 |
| Nonprod: | Other | | |
| Fixed: | Manager | 1.0 | 1.0 |
| Fixed: | Unit Clerk | 1.0 | 1.0 |
| Total FTEs 7-3 | | 7.1 | 10.2 |

| 3-11 Positions | | Daily | Total |
|---|---|---|---|
| Flex: | RN | 2.0 | 2.8 |
| Flex: | LPN | 1.0 | 1.4 |
| Flex: | Aide | 1.0 | 1.4 |
| Nonprod: | RN | | |
| Nonprod: | Other: LPN | .0 | .6 |
| Fixed: | Unit Clerk | 1.0 | 1.0 |
| Total FTEs 3-11 | | 5.0 | 7.2† |

| 11-7 Positions | | Daily | Total |
|---|---|---|---|
| Flex: | RN | 1.0 | 1.4 |
| Flex: | LPN | 1.0 | 1.4 |
| Flex: | Aide | .2 | .3 |
| Nonprod: | RN | | |
| Nonprod: | Other: LPN | .0 | .4 |
| Fixed: | | | |
| Total FTEs 11-7 | | 2.2 | 3.5† |

Form 4.1 - Example

† It is acceptable to make minor adjustments. Note changes from "Information" calculation above.

# Staffing Pattern

Department <u>North Wing</u>   Fiscal Year <u>1986</u>   Unit of Service <u>3.0 HPPD</u>
Flexible FTEs <u>15.9</u> Fixed FTEs <u>3.0</u> Nonproductive <u>2.0</u> Total FTEs <u>20.9</u>

## Staffing Pattern Information

| SHIFT | % OF WORK LOAD BY SHIFT | DIRECT CARE HOURS PER PT. DAY OR MODAL. | DAILY FTES |
|---|---|---|---|
| 7-3 | | | |
| 3-11 | | | |
| 11-7 | | | |
| 3-SHIFT TOTAL | 100% | | |

| FLEXIBLE (DIRECT) FTES | NON-PRODUCTIVE FTES | FIXED FTES | TOTAL FTES |
|---|---|---|---|
| | + | + | = |
| | + | + | = |
| | + | + | = |
| | | | |

## 7-3 Positions     Daily   Total

Flex: _____ _____ _____
Flex: _____ _____ _____
Flex: _____ _____ _____
Flex: _____ _____ _____
Nonprod: _____ _____ _____
Fixed: _____ _____ _____
Fixed: _____ _____ _____

**Total FTEs 7-3** _____ _____

## 3-11 Positions   Daily   Total

Flex: _____ _____ _____
Flex: _____ _____ _____
Flex: _____ _____ _____
Flex: _____ _____ _____
Nonprod: ____ _____ _____
Fixed: _____ _____ _____

**Total FTEs 3-11** _____ _____

## 11-7 Positions   Daily   Total

Flex: _____ _____ _____
Flex: _____ _____ _____
Flex: _____ _____ _____
Flex: _____ _____ _____
Nonprod: ____ _____ _____
Fixed: _____ _____ _____

**Total FTEs 11-7** _____ _____

# Staffing Pattern

Department _____ Fiscal Year _____ Unit of Service _____

Flexible FTEs ____ Fixed FTEs ____ Nonproductive FTEs ____ Total FTEs ____

## 7-3 Shift

| Position | Daily | Total |
|----------|-------|-------|
| Flex: | | |
| Flex: | | |
| Flex: | | |
| Flex: | | |
| Flex: | | |
| Nonprod: | | |
| Fixed: | | |
| Fixed: | | |
| **Total FTEs 7-3** | | |

## 3-11 Shift

| Position | Daily | Total |
|----------|-------|-------|
| Flex: | | |
| Flex: | | |
| Flex: | | |
| Flex: | | |
| Flex: | | |
| Nonprod: | | |
| Fixed: | | |
| Fixed: | | |
| **Total FTEs 3-11** | | |

## 11-7 Shift

| Position | Daily | Total |
|----------|-------|-------|
| Flex: | | |
| Flex: | | |
| Flex: | | |
| Flex: | | |
| Flex: | | |
| Nonprod: | | |
| Fixed: | | |
| Fixed: | | |
| **Total FTEs 11-7** | | |

Form 4.2 - Variation
page 45

# Section 5

# Prospective Budget Control

## Prospective Planning

Budgetary requests for staff or FTEs are approved through the allocation and assignment of funding. The approval implies a serious responsibility for the nurse manager to: (1) ensure delivery of the target level of quality and(2) achieve the target while spending no more than the allocated money. In a **fixed** budget system the salary budget remains constant regardless of changes in expected volume. If a nursing department was approved for $800,000 to pay the salaries of staff to take care of 8,000 patient days ($100 per patient day, on the average) and then only took care of 6,000 days, their costs per patient day would rise to $133 per patient day. If they took care of 10,000 patient days their costs would be reduced to $80 per patient day. In the fixed budget system, both of the above situations would be acceptable as long as annually no more or less than $800,000 was spent.

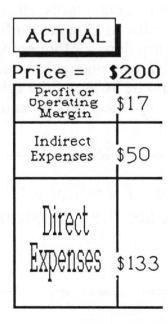

| BUDGET | | ACTUAL | |
|---|---|---|---|
| Price = $200 | | Price = $200 | |
| Profit or Operating Margin | $50 | Profit or Operating Margin | $17 |
| Indirect Expenses | $50 | Indirect Expenses | $50 |
| Direct Expenses | $100 | Direct Expenses | $133 |

However, in a **flexible**[4] budget system, the **$100 per patient day**, in the example, becomes the **target** to work toward, instead of the annual budget allotment. Those target dollars per patient day and the care HPPD become the budget constants and the desired goals to achieve. If the annual projected patient days were 6,000 with a budget allocation for $600,000 (@ $100 per patient day) and the actual census rose to 7,000 days, then the department could make an adjustment based on volume, called **volume adjusting**, to increase their spending to $700,000 because their target of $100 per patient day remains constant. Looking at the total and/or salary costs per patient day on a biweekly basis, along with the actual volume, is a good general indicator of budget control performance.

The purpose of this section is to demonstrate how to work with an approved budget by planning and monitoring prospectively to ensure on-target budget performance. Monthly reports that come out 6 weeks after the fact are useless except to reconfirm information the nurse manager already knows. It is far better to plan ahead, set up systems, and know each day that budget performance is on target. Two areas that influence achievement of budget targets are: (1) position control and (2) staff performance.

## External and Internal Variables

Variability is a norm in health care. Unpredictable swings in census or acuity can be a result of: (1) **external variables**, such as economic stability, technological advances, social mores, ethical trends or the political climate, and/or (2) **internal variables**, such as the infrastructure, availability of resources, or an organization's mission. Before embarking upon position control and the feedforward actions managers can take to control budgeted expenses, nurse managers should be aware of the following external and internal variables and consider how they affect quality and cost efficiency in their own organization.

---

"Nurses have a tendency to want to build parking lots to accommodate the Christmas rush."

- **George F. Nussbaum, RN, BSN**
OR/RR Supervisor, Wuerzburg, Germany

---

[4] The "semiflexible" model shown on page 26 is most often referred to as a "flexible" or "variable" budget system, with the common understanding that some element of that budget is fixed.

# External Variables

### Economic Variables:

Unstable Economy
Forced Competition
Cost-based to case-mix
    reimbursement
Cost accounting
Resource (3Ms: man/woman,
    materials, machinery) availability

### Political/Legal Variables:

Impact of partisan politics
Deregulation (or ultraregulation)
Prospective payment system
Malpractice

### Technological Variables:

Cost
Availability
Design focus on reducing cost of care
Advantages of technology:
    Monitoring capabilities
    Reduction of working hours
    Convenience
    More accurate clinical information
Disadvantages of technology:
    Expense
    Increased Manhours
    Obsolescence
    Quality of life issue

### Ethical Variables:

Quality of life issue
Personal value system conflicts
Health care access: right vs. privilege

### Social Variables:

Politics of health care organizations
Responsiveness of the hospital to changing
    demographics and social issues
Changing role of the hospital - controller
    to coordinator

# Internal Variables

### Resources (3 Ms):

Allocation
Availability
Demographics of staff
Staff mix

### Infrastructure:

Organization's mission statement
Organizational structure
Organizational goals and objectives
Policies and procedures

With so many different external variables affecting health care institutions in general and another multitude of internal variables affecting patient care and the internal management structure, the single-focused task of maintaining the budget sometimes can seem unattainable. If, however, the HPPD concept that has been proposed in the preceding pages of this workbook is maintained on a shift-by-shift basis, both short and long-range results will be attainable.

## Position Control

Budget planning and calculation are done, in part, to help manage a budget after it is approved. With competition in health care increasing, more and more attention will be paid to a manager's ability to control the department's budget and keep the budgeted labor HPPD in agreement with the budgeted target. When the final budget is approved for a particular number of FTEs (in the case of Section 3's workbook example, 20.9 were approved in total), those FTEs become the department **position control**, or the number of FTEs that can be on the payroll at any one given time. This is an important number to remember. The census will go up and down, and so will the acuity, and as a result the number of staff scheduled will go up and down accordingly. However, the position control remains rigidly constant throughout the fiscal year unless there is a mid-year, volume-based adjustment approved after several months of demonstrated volume increase. Even after the approval, the increase should be conservative as the census always seems to dive the day after additional staff members are hired to meet previously documented increased volume.

A very important step in managing the personnel budget is the decision to resist the temptation to overhire.

On the following pages the **Position Control Form**, Form **5.1**, is shown in two different ways: (1) Form 5.1-Example is filled in as it would be on a nursing unit, with a code for the legend on the page following it, and (2) Form 5.1 is a blank copy suitable for copying and implementation.

# Position Control Form

Footnotes to encircled numbers are on the following page.

| Position Title | Hours | FTE | Name-1 | Name-2 | Name-3 |
|---|---|---|---|---|---|
| RN | 2080 | 1.0 | J. Jones | | |
| RN | 2080 | 1.0 | ~~C. Hunt~~ | M. Fushmann ③ | |
| RN (Modified Full-time) ① | 1664 | .8 | J. Karaboyas | | |
| RN (Nonproductive) | 416 | .2 | Y. Kieval (PD) ④ | | |
| RN (Nonproductive) | 416 | .2 | S. Todaro (PD) | | |
| RN (Nonproductive) ② | 416 | .2 | D. Kranz (PD) | | |
| RN (Nonproductive) | 416 | .2 | V. Casey (PD) | | |
| RN (Nonproductive) | 416 | .2 | L. Laher (PD) | | |
| LPN | 2080 | 1.0 | F. Drury (RN) ⑤ | | |
| LPN | 832 | .4 | B. Blair (.5) ⑥ | | |
| Aide | 2080 | 1.0 | D. Russell | | |
| Aide | 2080 | 1.0 | B. Drew | | |
| Aide | 2080 | 1.0 | T. Kirk | | |
| Unit Clerk | 2080 | 1.0 | Pam Von | | |
| Manager | 2080 | 1.0 | C. Dison | | |

**7-3 SHIFT TOTAL** = 7.2 Flexible (Direct) + 1.0 Nonproductive + 2.0 Fixed = **10.2 Total 7-3 FTES**

| Position Title | Hours | FTE | Name-1 | Name-2 | Name-3 |
|---|---|---|---|---|---|
| RN | 2080 | 1.0 | B. Thomas | | |
| RN | 1044 | .5 | B. Ten Pas | | |
| RN | 1044 | .5 | T. Chris | | |
| RN | 1044 | .5 | J. Shlafer | | |
| RN | 626 | .3 | R. Johnston | | |
| LPN | 2080 | 1.0 | E. McClure | | |
| LPN | 832 | .4 | M. Meghan | | |
| LPN (Nonproductive) | 1248 | .6 | Do Not Fill ⑦ | | |
| Aide | 1044 | .5 | J. Greenfield | | |
| Aide | 1044 | .5 | J. Greenfield | | |
| Aide | 832 | .4 | A. Lawrence | | |
| Unit Clerk | 2080 | 1.0 | J. Thomas | | |

**3-11 SHIFT TOTAL** = 5.6 Flexible (Direct) + .6 Nonproductive + 1.0 Fixed = **7.2 Total 3-11 FTES**

| Position Title | Hours | FTE | Name-1 | Name-2 | Name-3 |
|---|---|---|---|---|---|
| RN | 2080 | 1.0 | M. Morrell | | |
| RN | 832 | .4 | ~~D. Blair~~ | ~~D. Michael~~ | ⑧ |
| LPN | 2080 | 1.0 | J. Peterson | | |
| LPN | 832 | .4 | T. Dunaye | | |
| LPN (Nonproductive) | 832 | .4 | Do Not Fill | | |
| Aide | 626 | .3 | Do Not Fill | | |

**11-7 SHIFT TOTAL** = 3.1 Flexible (Direct) + .4 Nonproductive + .0 Fixed = **3.5 Total 11-7 FTES**

⑨ **DEPARTMENT TOTAL FTES = 20.9**

Form 5.1 - Example

# Footnotes: Position Control Form (Form 5.1 - Example)

The example on the preceding page shows how the **Position Control Form**, Form **5.1**, can be used to help manage the hiring of personnel within approved budget constraints. The circled numbers correspond to the numbers below.

1. If there is a program to hire **full-time staff for less than a 40-hour week,** (a 32-hour week is used in this example), only the guaranteed hours should be reflected in the position control because any additional hours would be a result of increased volume and corresponding revenue.

2. **Nonproductive** hours should be separated and identified on the Position Control Form so they are not confused with direct care hours/FTE and as a reminder to preschedule vacations evenly throughout the fiscal year.

3. When **positions turn over,** the name of the employee who left should be eliminated, and the new hire's name should be recorded.

4. **Per diem (PD) staff** are scheduled to work only when needed and who can be called off at the last minute if census declines. They have few or no employee benefits and sometimes are employed by an outside agency.

5. Notation of an employee being hired into a position with a job description different than her own. In the example, an **RN was hired into an LPN position,** and the overage will show up in dollars, but not hours. This would probably require administrative approval and should be noted.

6. Occasionally staff are **hired to work more hours than the budgeted position** has available. In the example, a .5 part-time employee was hired into a .4 opening. It might have been done to help cover for a vacancy elsewhere in the budget, but whatever the reason, it should be noted for future reference.

7. The decision was made to **use per diem staff to cover nonproductive** time off. One full-time person could not possibly cover benefit days or unexpected absences with as much flexibility and cost efficiency.

8. A blank space or a name with a line through it reflects a position that has been **vacated** by an employee termination **and not yet refilled.** This might be a result of either an inability to find an appropriate replacement or possibly a manager reacting to a lower than budgeted (anticipated) census.

9. The sum of the 7-3, 3-ll and 11-7 shift's total FTEs.

# Position Control Form

| Position Title | Hours | FTE | Name-1 | Name-2 | Name-3 |
|---|---|---|---|---|---|
| | | | | | |
| | | | | | |
| | | | | | |
| | | | | | |
| | | | | | |
| | | | | | |
| | | | | | |
| | | | | | |
| | | | | | |
| | | | | | |
| | | | | | |
| | | | | | |

**7-3 SHIFT TOTAL =**

| | | | | | |
|---|---|---|---|---|---|
| | | | | | |
| | | | | | |
| | | | | | |
| | | | | | |
| | | | | | |
| | | | | | |
| | | | | | |
| | | | | | |
| | | | | | |
| | | | | | |
| | | | | | |

**3-11 SHIFT TOTAL =**

| | | | | | |
|---|---|---|---|---|---|
| | | | | | |
| | | | | | |
| | | | | | |
| | | | | | |
| | | | | | |

**11-7 SHIFT TOTAL =**          **DEPARTMENT TOTAL FTES =**

# Performance Appraisal Systems: Personnel's Role in Prospective Budget Control

Once position controls are in place the next challenge to the nurse manager lies in recruiting, selecting, and hiring the staff best able to meet the quality and budgetary goals. Traditional benefits of the performance appraisal process are fairly well known; however, this process is also very useful as a way to: (1) prospectively manage budget control activities by using job descriptions and evaluation criteria to negotiate several kinds of formal prehiring agreements and to (2) facilitate initial and ongoing communication of job responsibilities and standards that are designed to provide prospective and ongoing budget control.

The duties, responsibilities, expectations of performance, and the standards that will be used for evaluation allow prospective candidates to make an informed decision about their fit with the organization. Job descriptions and performance evaluations that are criteria-based and developed according to standards of expected performance provide prospective employees with a clear understanding of their duties, responsibilities, and evaluation criteria. This type of performance appraisal process has replaced the "trait" or "character" type of job description or evaluation:

## Approaches to Describing Skills and Competencies

| Trait | Criteria-Based |
|---|---|
| Handles stress well | Maintains predetermined level of performance when under stress |
| Telemetry experience | Able to operate telemetry equipment unassisted and interpret results |
| CPR certified and code experience | Assesses and, when necessary, initiates approved procedures for patients in cardiopulmonary arrest |

# Job Standards Provide
# Prospective and Ongoing Budget Control

The overall budgetary savings result from carefully constructed job responsibilities and performance standards.[5] Generally, employees who know what is expected of them in terms of results and who have a verifiable, measurable goal to work toward are usually successful. Thus, if cost containment is an important institutional goal, then the employee's responsibility for cost containment should be so stated, along with performance standards that identify measurable results for future evaluation based on those indicators. The last job responsibility described on the next page is one example of a cost-containment performance standard.

These examples demonstrate that any job duty or responsibility can be accompanied by a verifiable way of measuring whether or not the employee has met the standard, exceeded the standard, or needs to continue to work toward meeting it.[6] At the worst, the employee knows exactly what to do to improve and at what point performance will be acceptable. At the best, every employee knows exactly what is expected in terms of performance and can do a self-evaluation at any point of the year.

# Prehiring Agreements

Prehiring agreements are negotiations that take place with potential employees prior to hiring. Usually, this process includes reviewing the job description, policies, department procedures, and benefits. However, when job expectations and expected results are also defined and communicated to an employee during the initial interview in measurable, verifiable standards of performance, the benefits of prehiring agreements increase in a number of ways.

1. Having performance standards already defined and written allows candidates to decide before accepting the position if they are able and willing to work toward the position's prestated goals.

2. When position issues and responsibilities are discussed before hiring an employee, the interviewer and candidate can assess: (1) the compatibility of

---

[5] Also called **criteria statements** and **competency statements**.

[6] My thanks to Art Worth of Worth Developing, Largo, Florida, consultant and author of <u>Competency User Manual</u>, for introducing me to the "Meets the standard-Does not meet the standard-Exceeds the Standard" concept. He has freed me forever from words such as superior, meritorious, average and, the worst of all, below average.

| Job Responsibility | Performance Standard |
|---|---|
| DEVELOPS DISCHARGE PLANS FOR FAMILIES AND PATIENTS. | 1. utilizes knowledge of patient and hospital records to prepare discharge plan<br>2. utilizes knowledge of hospital and community service agencies to develop the plan and make referrals<br>3. develops discharge plan with physician consultation as needed<br>4. counsels and/or teaches patient and family on implementing the discharge plan |
| MAINTAINS SENSITIVITY TO THE PERSONAL NEEDS OF OTHERS. | 1. listens carefully and can restate the speaker's position on a given issue<br>2. describes the impact of decisions on those individuals who will be affected<br>3. demonstrates support and respect for others and their views, actively listening to others talk without interrupting and responding appropriately<br>4. addresses others tactfully on sensitive issues |
| PLANS AND COORDINATES THE UNIT WORKLOAD, ORGANIZING TO MAXIMIZE UTILIZATION OF RESOURCES. | 1. details plan for accomplishing unit goals<br>2. budgets, allocates staff as per budget and classified hours per patient day (HPPD)<br>3. sets priorities as per goal plan, reviewing periodically for revision<br>4. defines targets and establishes a control system with verifiable measures for manager evaluation<br>5. monitors, comparing actual results to target and taking corrective action as needed<br>6. communicates at each of the above steps to ensure clarity and purpose |
| SUPPORTS UNIT COST CONTAINMENT GOALS. | 1. records all patient charges during the shift used<br>2. completes patient care assignment within the 8-hour shift or confers with the nurse manager as soon as an overload is apparent<br>3. meets annual departmental attendance standards:<br>_0_ absences without notification<br>_4_ late/tardy occurrences<br>_4_ excused absence (1 major illness =1 incidence) |

their nursing practice philosophies and (2) the potential for agreement on or support of organizational and management goals. If the candidate accepts the position then he or she will enter into the new position with documented knowledge of the manager's expectations, thereby giving the new union the best chance for success and longevity.

3. The nurse manager can then use either the job description and/or corresponding performance evaluation as a written contractual agreement to confirm and document the prehiring agreement, giving one copy to the employee and including a copy in the new employee's personnel file.

4. Advance knowledge of what to expect from a job can significantly reduce the incidence of unpleasant and conflict-producing surprises after the employee is hired. With this approach, the manager and the new employee have an opportunity, before the hire, to clarify organizational goals, review personal employee goals, and assess them for compatibility.

## Pre-Hiring Agreement: Skill Level

Performance standards are also helpful in rating applicants for their starting salary rate and can help control the budget by paying increased dollars only when increased responsibilities are ensured. When hiring, the goal is to offer a position and salary commensurate with the stated level of performance. Skills do vary, however, and one ICU charge nurse may have significantly different experiences than another. Performance standards and corresponding skill check lists can help define the individual's experiences, skills and knowledge of the specialty to determine a fair and appropriate beginning salary that is compatible with the salaries of those already working within the system.

## Prehiring Agreement: Orientation

Orientation costs are another area of potential cost savings and budget control emanating from a good performance appraisal system. Several issues should be considered in relation to controlling orientation costs. First, each turnover of a position generates an orientation cost that varies according to the skill level of the new individual. Thus, reducing turnover can also reduce orientation costs.

Second, negotiating orientation costs at the time of hiring can be a positive cost control method. Given that the orientation will provide sufficient time for new staff members to become comfortable in their position, based on their stated skill level, it could also carry a cost limit. For example, new employees who achieved their targeted performance standards within the designated orientation time would be paid for 100 percent of their orientation costs but those who took twice as long to do so might only be paid for 50 percent (or some other negotiated figure), thus encouraging achievement, not failure.

Third, new graduate nurse (GN) orientation, which lasts from 4 weeks to 4 months, is another area that can benefit budgetarily from prehiring agreements based on job descriptions and/or performance evaluations. The length of orientation depends on the institution, chosen work unit, and the amount of expected responsibility. Performance standards can identify when the GN is ready to work independently, which may be sooner than the preplanned orientation period.

Traditionally, nursing has been willing to assume the financial responsibility of paying full salary to the orientee, but because of current cost constraints, some institutions have had to consider other alternatives. One alternative is cost sharing by the employee and/or the nursing school. For example, a new graduate requires a longer orientation period in order to be competent to provide care in an ICU. Because nursing curricula are unable to provide the extensive knowledge base required for working in an ICU nursing schools may be willing to assume or share the additional costs involved in placing and training their new graduates in these areas. Another option is to include a portion of orientees' hours as part of the direct care hours given to the shift that they work. Doing so will not change the actual work that they accomplish, but there would be some documentation that they participated in a revenue producing activity and the direct care HPPD would be reflected more accurately.

Prehiring agreements can take any form that the nursing management team wants them to, provided that incoming staff, established staff, and management are satisfied with the fairness and validity of the system. **Form 5.2-Example** is one format that can be used to document in writing an agreement with a new employee. By using the job description as a resource, new employees can self-evaluate, compare their actual level of performance to the evaluation criteria, and then identify those areas that need improvement. The first job responsibility shown on page 56, discharge planning, is used as an example of the form. Areas that do not meet the standard are prioritized, with target dates for further development and accomplishment. The target dates vary depending on the need for the skill; when immediate expertise is essential, the nurse manager might even require that the new employee meet all of the criteria statements of the performance evaluation prior to the end of orientation or even prior to hiring.

Prehiring agreements are negotiations, and if negotiated carefully and fairly, both management and the new employee will have a similar vision of what is

## Prehire Agreement and Documentation Format

Employee _____

| Area of Performance that did not Meet the Standard | Expected Results | Corrective Action to be taken | Target Date |
|---|---|---|---|
| Development of the discharge plan for families and patients. | Employee will meet the stated performance standard or achieve skill proficiency in the following areas: *<br><br>1. Become familiar with patient and hospital records, hospital and community service agencies, and the process of consulting with physicians.<br><br>2. Uses all of the above information to develop the discharge plan and make referrals.<br><br>3. Able to counsel and/or teach patient and family how to implement the discharge plan. | 1. Orient 2 hours in Medical Records.<br><br>2. Attend a half day discharge planning workshop.<br><br>3. Review all discharge planning policies and procedures.<br><br>4. Initiate and complete an entire discharge planning process under the observation of a preceptor for the purpose of evaluation. | End of Orientation Period. |

Employee Signature _____

Manager Signature _____

* This can be footnoted to the job description and performance evaluation, and restated here for documentation purposes.

Form 5.2-Example

## Prehire Agreement and Documentation Format

Employee _____

| Area of Performance that did not Meet the Standard | Expected Results | Corrective Action to be taken | Target Date |
|---|---|---|---|
| | | | |

Employee Signature _____

Manager Signature _____

expected to be accomplished. Because the job description describes the duties and responsibilities of the employee and the performance evaluation describes the criteria that will be used to evaluate performance, the combination of the two become valuable measures and commitments for prehiring agreements with benefits that continue after hiring that are consistent with other ongoing staff agreements.

In summary, the budget control benefits of the the performance appraisal system are three-fold:

1. As a prehiring tool it can be used as a self-assessment measure and a commitment from new employees that they can meet an acceptable level of performance.

2. As an ongoing management tool it continues to provide incentives that motivate staff to achieve organizational goals while concurrently working toward personal achievement.

3. Employees who know what is expected, and how to get there, are usually satisfied and tend to have positive performance evaluations. They tend to be employed for the long term, which reduces expensive turnover and orientation costs. And last, they can have the incentive, via their performance appraisal system, to look within their department to discover what can be done better for the sake of quality and what can be done faster to enhance productivity.

# Section 6

# Prescheduling Staff-
# More Planning Ahead

## Preschduling-The Last Plan

Prescheduling for daily staffing of personnel is the greatest challenge facing nurse managers today. In order to achieve the staffing goals set forth in the budget plan, the nurse manager must take appropriate action throughout the fiscal year toward achieving that goal. Nurse managers are responsible and accountable for this planning task, which begins with developing unit standard hours per patient day (HPPD) or per modality and continues with the budget process and prescheduling of staff. Prescheduling of staff enables the unit to maximize both quality and productivity by adequately preparing ahead, proactively, for the unknown census and acuity levels of future patients. Prescheduling, through the preparation of time sheets for staff schedules and the daily reallocation of staff to meet classified care requirements of that day, must satisfy three diverse but equally important criteria: (1) quality of patient care, (2) cost containment or budgetary constraints, and (3) staff preference.

## Quality of Patient Care

The quality of nursing care directly contributes to the patient's condition and recovery. It is the foremost concern of all nurses, from the new graduate to the chief executive nurse. Past assessments of quality were frequently based on time availability, i.e. the more time available for patient care, the higher the quality of care delivered. The current emphasis on outpatient care is effectively shortening inpatient stays and, at the same time, increasing the care hours required by remaining inpatients. Thus, in order to maintain the desired level of quality while still meeting cost-containment goals, appropriate nursing staff must be matched to the required care needs of the patients.

## Cost Containment

Cost containment is no longer a voluntary option. In the old days (last year), a nurse manager could identify the average acuity and hours needed per patient day and budget the dollars for those hours for the upcoming fiscal year. Today, hours per patient day (HPPD) are often mandated by the hospital as a result of financial distress, budgetary constraints, or government controls. In addition, traditional third party payers, HMOs and PPOs are also limiting care hour availability to patients through their negotiations for deep discounts and reduced payments to the institutions for their services. The end result: less available money to pay for the nursing care hours to the patient at the same time that the average patient care hours required and nursing salaries are increasing. There is now a very limited amount of money to deliver patient care; the successful nurse managers and nurse administrators are going to be the ones who are able to contain costs while at the same time achieving and enhancing quality by examining the prestated standard level of care and available hours and asking, "How can we do this faster and better?"

## Staff Preference

When thoughtfulness is demonstrated to the nursing staff, it will be reciprocated in the future when the nurse manager has unexpected or extraordinary needs. The level of rapport and consideration that management and the professional staff have for one another enhances the quality of care and increases productivity through the efforts of a satisfied and motivated staff working toward the achievement of organizational objectives.

## Reallocation: Staff, Quality, Cost

Daily staffing decisions and reallocations must meet the three criteria above to ensure the effective management of the nursing unit. As the nurse manager examines the classification levels and volume of patients in the individual units, she may find it necessary to make adjustments because of: (1) increased or decreased census, (2) increased or decreased acuity, or (3) unexpected staff absences. The daily adjustments help the nurse manager reallocate both nursing care hours and nursing dollars where they are needed so that the goal of optimal care at the lowest cost can be successfully pursued. Daily adjustments and reallocation of staff can work positively for both the institution and the staff member . . . a nurse who works 7-3/3-11, on a Thursday to cover for an ill co-worker can take Friday off and have a 3-day weekend as a bonus. It's not a simple task, but staff reallocation is certainly attainable with careful planning and proper preparation.

## Preplanning, Preparation, Process

Prescheduling and daily staffing of personnel can be the bane of the nurse manager's existence, or it can be a fair, efficient, and cost-effective system designed to meet the needs of the patients, the staff, and budget expectations. Careful planning and preparation must take place prior to the actual scheduling process to ensure optimal results.

---

### Staffing System Planning Process

- Organizational and unit objectives should focus on meeting the needs of the patients, the staff, and the budget.

- A nursing unit's primary objective is to provide a predetermined amount of time, on the average, to each patient each day of the stay.

- The dollars required to provide the following become the unit salary budget:

  (1) direct hours per patient day (HPPD)
  (2) nonproductive hours
  (3) fixed hours

- Unit goals, including the desired HPPD, are approved when required budget dollars are approved and allocated as requested.

- The unit goals should be clearly prioritized and communicated, along with an understanding that sometimes the priorities might change.

- Personnel and staffing policies must support the objectives, be mutually agreed to by all involved, and communicated verbally and in writing.

---

## Personnel and Staffing Policies

Policies for staffing and scheduling of personnel provide the backbone of successful staffing systems that ensure fair treatment, adequate coverage for patient care requirements, and cost-effective scheduling. Although each institution needs to develop and implement policies that meet its own individual needs, some familiar policies are described below.

---

# Sample Staffing Policies

- All licensed personnel will have 26 weekends off per year. Whenever possible, they will follow an every-other-weekend pattern.

- All requests will be granted in the order received, with the earliest date having priority. Exceptions:
    (1) emergency medical leave
    (2) winter holidays:
        - Each employee will be off either the Christmas or New Year's holiday.
        - Whatever holiday is worked one year will be guaranteed off the next year.
        - Trades will be approved by the nurse manager after everyone has been scheduled for one holiday off.

- All changes of scheduled days are to be written, approved, and signed by the nurse manager and turned into the staffing office. No overtime will be approved for changes.

- Required weekdays off can be guaranteed if the employee works every weekend.

- Once schedules are posted (2 weeks prior to the start of the period), no changes will be made without the permission of the employee.

- All summer vacation requests will be submitted to the nurse manager by April 1st.

---

Once policies are agreed upon[7], written and communicated to all staff through unit meetings and pre-employment interviews, they serve as a reference for all staffing related decisions and provide guidelines for equal treatment of all employees. Further, they serve as an employee reference document that outlines what is expected from the employee, and as importantly, what the employee can expect and count on from management.

---

[7] Staff ad hoc (or "self-destruct" committees) are an excellent methodology for developing or revising staffing policies. Also, it is a good idea to have each employee sign a copy of the staffing policies. One copy should remain in the personnel file, and the other copy should be retained by the employee for future reference.

## Planning Ahead for Vacations and Other Prescheduled Absences

Vacations and other special requests for time off are another area that needs to be considered prior to preparing the the time sheet schedules if there is to be an even balance between the needs of the patients, the needs of the staff and the needs of the budget. The **Vacation Scheduling** memos (Illustrations **6.1** and **6.2**) and **Request For Days Off** form (Form **6.4**) are excellent tools that will assist the individual responsible for preparing the schedules. However, planning ahead is really the key here. If the nurse manager has all the requests in hand when preparing the schedules, she can arrange the schedule so each can be granted. If a request comes in at the last minute, after other's days off have been promised, she can only refer the individual to co-workers for a trade or call off in the event of an unexpected low census. Here are some ideas that might be integrated into a special request policy:

# Policy Issues: Requests for Days Off

- Encourage staff to plan as far ahead as possible to facilitate approval of their requests.

- Require requests be turned in by the time the schedules are started. After that time a trade will have to be made with a co-worker.

- Grant requests in the order they are received.

- Encourage or require vacation requests, especially summer ones, well in advance to enable staff to coordinate their approved vacation with their family.

- Notify staff as soon as possible about the outcome of their requests.

- Keep records of requested days off, including those not granted, and who has had special holidays off. Monitor request activity and fairness of the requests.

- Take notice of the staff members who never ask for any days off, making sure they are getting some special holidays and choice days off once in a while.

- If the request cannot be granted, look for a negotiation or a partial granting and discuss it with the individual.

- Perhaps the most important thing for the nurse manager to keep in mind is that not every request can be granted.

Scheduling earned benefit time should be respected and acknowledged as something special, giving full effort to granting the staff member's first or second choice for time off. Staff members work hard to earn 2 to 3 weeks off with their families, and vacation time is one way the institution can reward them and demonstrate genuine concern and good will. With careful preplanning by both management and staff, this becomes an attainable goal and can usually be achieved without compromising the other two goals of patient care and cost containment.

## Basic Scheduling Techniques

Prescheduling staff through the preparation of time sheets is a time-consuming task, but it can be extremely satisfying to both the staff and the unit when done properly, and sometimes it can even be fun. This section is written so that a novice can use it to learn this skill, but even the pros will probably pick up a tip or two and can use this as a reference for teaching new managers. Here is a list of the information that should be known by the manager before preparing the schedules:

---

## Prescheduling Information to Know

- standard of care: budgeted direct hours of care per patient day (HPPD)

- staffing pattern for the average projected census and approved staffing mix (number of RNs, LPNs, etc.)

- staffing policies

- skill levels of staff: ability for relief charge, years of experience, etc.

- number of days that part-time personnel work per week

- availability of per diem personnel: how much they'll work and when

- individual staff idiosyncracies: it can give the schedules a personal touch and meet everyone's needs more often. For example, if Jan asks for every Monday off to volunteer at her child's school, maybe she'd rather cover 3-11 on Mondays and save her day off for herself.

---

# The Scheduling Process Step-by-Step

Once the above information is known or at hand for future reference, the task can be simplified by following a routine procedure using the example below:

1. On the **Two Week Staff Schedule**, (Form **5.2**), write in the employee's (a) name, (b) position and (c) the FTE hours hired to work. If working with a large unit, it may be desirable to put one shift on each page.

2. Indicate normal weekend off with "X's" on each day off and dashes "--" for days on (...a pencil with an eraser is always recommended for use with scheduling). Note: Lee and Hart traded weekends on the 14th to accommodate Hart's vacation.

3. If an employee is on the weekend that the time sheet begins, such as D. Blair, make a note of her last day off (noted here in the Monday, January 2 column) to eliminate the chance of unintentionally scheduling too long a stretch on duty.

4. Work done on the staffing pattern development is carried over in prescheduling actual staff members to meet both patient volume and acuity needs. Direct, fixed, and nonproductive FTEs are broken down on the pattern and should be separated on the schedule as well. Albert is filling the nonproductive FTE, and fixed FTE have been omitted entirely for this exercise.[8] The purpose of this action is to be a reminder to: (a) schedule benefit time each pay period and (b) diminish the urge to add the nonproductive or fixed hours into the direct care hours, which would reduce available hours for vacation, holiday coverage, and indirect care. Although Albert is covering a weekend, the 7th and 8th, which is not benefit time, the per diem employee, Kieval will end up covering the two additional 2 benefit days.

Shift _7-3_
Pay Period Ending _1-14-86_

Two-Week Staff Sche

| NAME POSITION - FTE | sun Jan 1 | mon 2 | tue 3 | wed 4 | thu 5 | fri 6 | sat 7 | sun 8 | mon 9 | tue 10 | wed 11 | thu 12 | fri 13 | sat 14 |
|---|---|---|---|---|---|---|---|---|---|---|---|---|---|---|
| J.Jones *RN-1.0 FTE* | X | | | | | | — | — | | | | | | X |
| D.Blair *RN-1.0 FTE* | — | W | | | | | X | X | | | | | | — |
| C.Todaro *RN-1.0 FTE* | — | Th | | | | | X | X | | | | | | — |
| N.Lee *RN - .5 FTE* | X | | | | | | — | — | | | | | | — |
| V.Hart *RN - .5 FTE* | — | F | | | | | X | X | | | | | | X |
| Y.Kieval *RN - .2 FTE* | X | | | | | | X | X | | | | | | X |
| | | | | | | | | | | | | | | |
| B.Rink *LPN-1.0 FTE* | X | | | | | | — | — | | | | | | X |
| E.Mack *LPN-.4 FTE* | — | W | | | | | X | X | | | | | | — |
| | | | | | | | | | | | | | | |
| F.Albert *LPN-.6 FTE* | X | | | | | | — | — | | | | | | X |
| | 4 | | | | | | 4 | 4 | | | | | | 4 |

---

[8] Note that this example does not follow the example on pages 40-42 as the large number of FTEs involved would make it more complicated.

5. Make a note in "Comments" section of the benefit time due to be taken as a reminder to the employee and the person completing the schedules.

6. Write in all requests for time off, on, or to other shifts with an "R" ($X^R$, $\text{--}^R$, 11-7$^R$) as a reminder to all that this is a request. If holidays and vacation days are sometimes assigned, then requested ones should also be marked with an "R" so that it is not forgotten when the schedules are being prepared, and also to remind the manager when the period arrives that these are special days off and not to call for extra shift coverage. Assume at this point that all requests can be granted, but also make a note in the "Comments" section of the request date (shown in the example as "12/1" and "11/2") in case requests are more plentiful than available time off.

7. If staff need to be rotated to another shift to cover a key vacancy, do it at this point so you can give them a preference for days off. Some staff like their day off the day before rotating to 3-11 rather than after, stating that if they're tired the following day, they'd rather be at work. At times shift rotation is mandatory[9] and the scheduling person can't change that fact, but they can make the chore as pleasant or as palatable as possible. Note also that by the time the schedules are done, the per diem RN will be working 2 days to cover benefit time and 2 extra days to cover the hours required to cover vacant positions on other shifts.

| | | Shift 7-3 — Pay Period Ending 1-14-86 | | | | | | | Two-Week Staff Schedule | | | | | | |
|---|---|---|---|---|---|---|---|---|---|---|---|---|---|---|---|
| Day | sun | mon | tue | wed | thu | fri | sat | sun | mon | tue | wed | thu | fri | sat | |
| NAME / Date | Jan 1 | 2 | 3 | 4 | 5 | 6 | 7 | 8 | 9 | 10 | 11 | 12 | 13 | 14 | Comments |
| RN-1.0 FTE | X | | | | | | — | — | | | | | | X | Hol |
| RN-1.0 FTE | — | | | | | | $X^R$ | $X^R$ | Hol | | | | | — | ~~Hol~~ 12/1 |
| RN-1.0 FTE | — | | | | $X^R$ | Vac | $X^R$ | $X^R$ | | | | | | — | 11/2 |
| RN -.5 FTE | X | 11-7 | $X^R$ | $X^R$ | | | — | — | | | | | | — | on 2, off 2 |
| RN -.5 FTE | — | X | $X^R$ | $X^R$ | $X^R$ | Vac | $X^R$ | $X^R$ | $X^R$ | $X^R$ | Vac | Vac | Vac | $X^R$ | off 2, on 2 |
| RN -.2 FTE | X | | $X^R$ | $3^R11$ | $X^R$ | | X | X | | | | | | X | Per Diem |
| | | | | | | | | | | | | | | | |
| LPN-1.0 FTE | X | | | | | | — | — | | | | | | X | 3 Vac |
| LPN-.4 FTE | — | | | | | | X | X | | | | | | — | |
| | | | | | | | | | | | | | | | |
| LPN-.6 FTE | X | | | | | | — | — | | | | | | X | Nonprod. |
| | 4 | 4 | 4 | 4 | 4 | 4 | 4 | 4 | 4 | 4 | 4 | 4 | 4 | 4 | |

---

[9] If rotations are needed, or any other unpleasant assignments, for that matter, are required, make sure assignments are fair and equitable. Even if staff members trade 11-7s for weekends off, let them make the trade after the schedules are posted. The posted schedules should always demonstrate absolute equality for rotations, floats, etc., and records should be kept in order to document assignments.

8. Start giving the remaining staff their days off, leaving the part-timers for last,because their days are more flexible.  Keep counting as you move along, making sure the number of staff, staff mix, and skill strengths is remaining even.  Prescheduling the 4 staff daily leaves this unit in the best position to react as quickly as possible to high or low census and high or low acuities.  The day that only 3 are prescheduled will inevitably be the day the census skyrockets with very ill patients and the manager will be searching for two extra staff instead of one.

9. Review individually with staff any time changes are made that are out of the ordinary, such as a change in routine weekend off or a change in a routine rotation to another shift.

10. Finally, post the schedules at least 2 weeks prior to the start of the period.  Be available for comments, corrections, etc., and if there's a manager error. . . fix it fast!

Shift __7-3__
Pay Period Ending __1-14-86__

# Two-Week Staff Schedule

| NAME | Day / Date | sun Jan 1 | mon 2 | tue 3 | wed 4 | thu 5 | fri 6 | sat 7 | sun 8 | mon 9 | tue 10 | wed 11 | thu 12 | fri 13 | sat 14 | Comments |
|---|---|---|---|---|---|---|---|---|---|---|---|---|---|---|---|---|
| RN-1.0 FTE | | X | — | — | — | — | X | — | — | — | — | X | — | — | X | Hol |
| RN-1.0 FTE | | — | X | — | — | — | — | X$^R$ | X$^R$ | Hol | — | — | — | X | — | Hol 12/1 |
| RN-1.0 FTE | | — | — | — | — | X$^R$ | Vac | X$^R$ | X$^R$ | — | — | — | X | — | — | 11/2 |
| RN-.5 FTE | | X | 11-7 | X$^R$ | X$^R$ | — | X | — | — | X | X | X | X | X | — | on 2, off 2 |
| RN-.5 FTE | | — | X | X$^R$ | X$^R$ | X$^R$ | Vac | X$^R$ | X$^R$ | X$^R$ | X$^R$ | Vac | Vac | Vac | X$^R$ | off 2, on 2 |
| RN-.2 FTE | | X | — | X$^R$ | 3$^R$11 | X | — | X | X | — | X | X | X | X | X | Per Diem |
| | | | | | | | | | | | | | | | | |
| LFN-1.0 FTE | | X | — | — | X | — | — | — | — | X | — | — | — | — | X | 3 Vac |
| LFN-.4 FTE | | — | X | X | — | X | X | X | X | — | X | X | X | X | — | |
| | | | | | | | | | | | | | | | | |
| LFN-.6 FTE | | X | X | X | X | X | — | — | — | X | X | — | — | — | X | Nonprod. |
| | | 4 | 4 | 4 | 4 | 4 | 4 | 4 | 4 | 4 | 4 | 4 | 4 | 4 | | |

Adjustments should be made to complement individual personnel policies and routines of the specific units involved.  Success depends on communication, fairness,and adherence to the budgetary plan, for it is imperative that cost guidelines and the desired level of patient care not be compromised at the expense of staff preference.

## Priorities and Scheduling

As stated previously, within each staffing system there are three key issues: (1) quality of care, including numbers and mix of staff needed to achieve the desired quality, (2) cost containment, and (3) staff preference. It is not always possible to meet all of these goals, so it is essential that nurse managers at all levels in an organization identify the priorities of the department, agree on their priorities, and agree on when exceptions should and should not be made. Flexibility in prescheduling and daily reallocations will be a real asset to the nurse manager. Here are some examples:

---

### It's **OK** To Be Flexible

Preschedule less staff during the summer months to accommodate more vacation scheduling, as long as other staff agree to carry the extra load in the event of an unexpected high census.

The nurse manager may elect to staff short over the winter holiday season when a predictably low census is expected.

On selected days, when department projects, policies, or planning activities are scheduled, the nurse manager may preschedule extra staff. If this is planned for properly, it can be achieved without compromising budget targets.

---

Even the most cost-conscious manager needs the flexibility to make a decision that may not be the most cost effective, but that allow one of the other goals of patient care or staff preference to be met successfully. Although sound planning provides the basis for effective allocation of staff, the nurse manager must use judgment and experience to set priorities and make decisions.

# Vacation Scheduling Letter

Date: _____
Start of Fiscal Year

To:        Nursing Staff

From:      Head Nurse

Subject:   Vacation Scheduling

As of _____ (date) you are eligible for _____ (number) vacation days, to be taken anytime within this fiscal year beginning _____ and ending _____ . Please consult your personnel handbook to double check my calculations and if you have any questions, call me at ext.#_____ . It is your responsibility to keep track of your vacation days and check your paycheck stub to see that you have been properly paid. If you wish to double check remaining vacation time, please call at the number above.

P.S. - Don't forget to submit summer (May-September) vacation requests by March l5th and all other vacation requests 6-8 weeks in advance.

# Vacation Memo

To:        All Department Staff

From:      Head Nurse

Subject:  Vacation Scheduling


1. Vacation requests are due to the Head Nurse 6-8 weeks in advance or by March l5th for summer vacations (May-Sept.).  Summer LOA requests by part-time and full-time employees who have not yet earned vacation are also due by March l5th.

2. If there are too many vacation requests for one period of time, the individual with the latest date on request (i.e. first come, first serve) will be contacted, and an attempt will be made to plan another compatible date.  The best way to avoid a conflict, in advance, is to look at the board in the department to see what has already been requested and what's been approved. No more than one RN, one LPN or one nursing aide can be away at the same time.

3. In order that the employee will have time to make his or her vacation plans, the written approval of the request will be returned as soon as possible (not to exceed 1 month).

4. Changes in an approved vacation require that a written request be submitted to the HN.  It will be processed as a new request.

5. After all vacation requests are processed, employees who are eligible for vacation but have not submitted a request will be contacted and an available time will be recommended.  If the employee does not have a preference, an assignment will be made that is agreeable to both the employee and the department.

6. Advance vacation pay requests are due 4 weeks prior to the start of vacation.

7. Please keep in mind that vacation scheduling may affect the way your weekends are scheduled, but not their total number.

# Vacation Schedule

Department _____    Year _____

| Month | Jan | Feb | Mar | Apr | May | June | July | Aug | Sept | Oct | Nov | Dec |
|-------|-----|-----|-----|-----|-----|------|------|-----|------|-----|-----|-----|
| Week Beginning: | | | | | | | | | | | | |
| Employee | | | | | | | | | | | | |
| | | | | | | | | | | | | |
| | | | | | | | | | | | | |
| | | | | | | | | | | | | |
| | | | | | | | | | | | | |
| | | | | | | | | | | | | |
| | | | | | | | | | | | | |
| | | | | | | | | | | | | |
| | | | | | | | | | | | | |
| | | | | | | | | | | | | |
| | | | | | | | | | | | | |
| | | | | | | | | | | | | |
| | | | | | | | | | | | | |
| | | | | | | | | | | | | |
| | | | | | | | | | | | | |
| | | | | | | | | | | | | |

# Request for Days Off

Unit: _____          Date: _____

Name: _____          Position: _____

Day/Date(s) of Requested Time Off[1]: _____

_____

_____

Pay:     _____ Sick Hours[2] _____ Regular Day Off
         _____ Vacation Hours _____ Holiday Hours
         _____ Other: Jury Duty, Military, Death, Medical, or Personal Leave
                   Describe _____

         _____

If this involves your normal weekend to work and you have made arrangements
with a co-worker to trade weekends, please state co-worker's name and have
them initial this form.

_____
[1] If you have a preference of how benefit days are to be scheduled, indicate here.
[2] Sick time may be prescheduled if the physician request is on file in Health Office.

Form 6.4
page 76

# Two-Week Staff Schedule

Department: **Med-Surg**
Shift: **All**
Pay Period Ending: **Jan. 14, 1986**

| Name – Position – FTE | | Sun 1/1 | Mon 2 | Tue 3 | Wed 4 | Thu 5 | Fri 6 | Sat 7 | Sun 8 | Mon 9 | Tue 10 | Wed 11 | Thu 12 | Fri 13 | Sat 14 | Comments |
|---|---|---|---|---|---|---|---|---|---|---|---|---|---|---|---|---|
| 1A 7-3/RN | 1.0 | X^R | – | – | – | – | X^R | – | – | – | – | X^R | – | – | X^R | |
| 2A 7-3/RN | 1.0 | – | X | – | – | – | – | X^R | X^R | – | – | – | – | X | – | |
| 3A 7-3/RN | 1.0 | X^R | – | – | – | X | – | – | – | X | – | – | – | HOL | X^R | |
| 4A 7-3/RN | 1.0 | – | – | X^R | X^R | – | X | X^R | X^R | X^R | X^R | X | – | – | – | |
| 5A 7-3/RN | 1.0 | – | – | 11-7 | X | – | HOL | X^R | X^R | 3-11 | – | – | X | – | – | |
| 6A 7-3/RN | .6 | X | X | – | – | X | – | X | X | X | X | – | X | – | X | |
| **TOTALS** | **5.6** | 3 | 4 | 4 | 4 | 4 | 4 | 3 | 3 | 4 | 4 | 4 | 4 | 4 | 3 | |
| 1B 3-11/RN | 1.0 | X^R | X^R | – | – | X | X | – | – | X | – | X | X | – | X^R | |
| 2B 3-11/RN | 1.0 | – | X | – | – | – | X | X^R | X^R | – | – | – | X | – | – | |
| 3B 3-11/RN | 1.0 | X^R | – | – | X^R | – | – | X^R | – | – | X | 3-11 | – | – | X^R | |
| 4B 3-11/RN | 1.0 | X^R | – | X | X | X | – | X^R | HOL | HOL | – | X | X | X | – | |
| 5B 3-11/RN | .5 | – | – | – | X | X | – | X^R | X^R | X | – | X | X | X | X^R | |
| 6B 3-11/RN | .5 | X | X | X | X | X | – | X^R | X^R | X | – | X | – | X | – | |
| 7B UNFILLED | .6 | | | | | | | | | | | | | | | |
| **TOTALS** | **5.6** | 3 | 4 | 4 | 4 | 4 | 4 | 3 | 3 | 4 | 4 | 4 | 4 | 4 | 3 | |
| 1C 11-7/RN | 1.0 | X^R | – | – | – | – | – | X^R | – | – | – | – | – | – | X^R | |
| 2C 11-7/RN | 1.0 | X^R | – | X^R | X^R | – | – | X^R | X^R | X^R | – | – | – | X^R | X^R | On 2 weekends, off 2 |
| 3C 11-7/RN | 1.0 | X^R | – | – | – | VAC | – | X^R | – | X | X | 3-11 | – | 3-11 | X^R | |
| 4C 11-7/RN | 1.0 | – | – | X | – | VAC | X | X^R | – | – | – | X | X | – | – | |
| 5C 11-7/RN | 1.0 | – | X | VAC | VAC | VAC | – | – | – | – | – | – | – | 3-11 | – | |
| 6C 11-7/RN | .6 | X^R | X^R | VAC | – | – | X^R | X^R | X^R | – | X | – | X | X | – | Off 2 weekends, on 2 |
| **TOTALS** | **5.6** | 3 | 4 | 4 | 4 | 4 | 4 | 3 | 3 | 4 | 4 | 4 | 4 | 4 | 3 | |

Form 6.5 – Example

# Two–Week Staff Schedule

Department _____

Shift _____

Pay Period Ending _____

| Day and Date: | Sun | Mon | Tue | Wed | Thu | Fri | Sat | Sun | Mon | Tue | Wed | Thu | Fri | Sat | Comments |
|---|---|---|---|---|---|---|---|---|---|---|---|---|---|---|---|
| Name – Position – FTE | | | | | | | | | | | | | | | |

# About the Author

Roey Kirk is a noted expert in nursing management. Using her own experiences from 11 years of working in managerial and administrative positions in a 513-bed community hospital, she has developed systems that organize and simplify the nursing management function.

As an adjunct university instructor of applied management, seminar leader, and consultant, Roey Kirk has helped many individuals and organizations make the most of their nursing staff. She believes that quality and productivity can exist side by side, and that nursing can make a positive impact on a hospital's profitability. Using time tested methods, candor and understanding she shows readers, students, and workshop participants that proactive management skills are not a gift that only some are born with, but a set of techniques that can be easily learned, immediately used, and adapted.

Roey Kirk holds a baccalaureate degree in sociology and a master's degree in management. She has written articles for nursing management journals, authored feature articles for a nurse executive tape series, and has lectured at many programs nationwide for nurse managers, administrators, and executives. She has published several other books on nursing management including, *Nursing Quality and Productivity: Practical Management Tools*. She owns her own management consulting firm, Roey Kirk Associates, in Miami, Florida.